OPEN
LETTER
TO
GOD

OPEN
LETTER
TO
GOD

by

ROBERT ESCARPIT

H
A **HEINEMAN** PAPERBACK

*Further books in this series
are in preparation by
American, British, French, German,
Italian and Spanish authors.*

FIRST PRINTING 1968
Translated from the French by Joseph M. Bernstein
Library of Congress Catalogue Card No. 68-10242
© 1966, Éditions Albin Michel, Paris, under the title
"Lettre ouverte à Dieu"
© 1967, James H. Heineman, Inc.,
60 East 42nd Street,
New York, N. Y. 10017

A FOREWORD

The Open Letter series was conceived and developed as the platform for an international assembly of prominent people and established writers to discuss, dissect and delve into contemporary ideas and mores.

Each Open Letter is addressed to a segment of modern society, but its audience is all of us who do not accept the inevitable; who are seeking and questioning; and who are not afraid of being jolted out of complacence. Each letter is written with irony and charm; with optimism spiked with skepticism; and with humor laced with wit. Each letter is a personal polemic in which the author appeals to the mind rather than to the emotions; and chides with the épée rather than bludgeons with the hammer.

Books by American authors in this series are appearing in translation in Europe and Latin America. Publishers in other countries are adding their own titles to the series, which will appear in translation in the United States. Hence, a consortium of international writers will present, in companion Open Letters, divergent views, but always in keeping with the concept of the Open Letter series.

OPEN
LETTER
TO
GOD

To my first fountain pen, and to all the secret and precious things that have been given me, especially the names of women, the last two of which are my granddaughters Isabelle and Nathalie.

NOTICE
to the Postmaster General

Dear Sir:

I am entrusting this letter to you without a stamp, and I suppose that the addressee will have to pay for postage due. He isn't stingy. I know him by reputation: If you waive the postal charges, he will reimburse you a hundred times over.

I am not putting any stamp on my letter because I don't know the postal rates for the Beyond. We have a general idea of what it costs to ship human beings there. There has never been any mystery about that information—from Charon's obol to the current rates charged by funeral homes. We also know that oral messages are theoretically free. All you have to do is to assume the proper moral and physical posture, then pronounce distinctly the text you want sent—using if possible one of the standard formulas the church authorities have made available to the public. This is not a must, but it

13

prevents mistakes and speeds up delivery. In some countries they even use ingenious prayer wheels, gadgets that transmit prayers like our "singing" telegrams.

But there are no regulations for written messages or, in general, for objects whether registered or not. The procedures for transmitting them are ill defined. They are burned, swallowed, tossed into the water—it depends on the religion or historical period in question. I wouldn't advise you to use any of these methods for my letter.

The only known precedent is that of Santa Claus. Every year children write to him and tell him what they want for Christmas. Some countries have even set up special post offices for receiving and opening this mail. Maybe that's an idea you yourself could work on. Still, the two are in rather different situations. There is no doubt that Santa Claus exists. As proof, I need only point out that a goodly number of the requests addressed to him are granted on December 25. We must therefore assume that they reached their destination.

But with God the problem is not the same. We have no statistics to show that the percentage of prayers granted runs above the fifty-percent mark. Not that the problem is a burning one. But I find it hard to ask you to mobilize your work force for a correspondent who may not even exist.

One solution might be to install special letter boxes in various places, paint them a heavenly blue, and then wait for a miracle. There is no reason why that might not succeed. Look at the poor boxes in churches. You drop your donation to God in them, and the money seems to reach its destination regularly. Anyhow, one never sees it again.

Then there is the question of an address. If worst comes to worst, you can forward my letter to Rome, Mecca, Jerusalem, or even to Tirana where my friend the Baba of the Bektashi-Moslems lives as supreme head of a religious community numbering several million followers. In each of these cities you will find accredited representatives of the one and only God. Unfortunately—and this is where the difficulty lies—we're not at all sure whether they represent the same God.

That is why, all things considered, I have preferred the device of an open letter. Of course under these circumstances I can hardly ask you to guarantee privacy for my correspondence. A lot of people are going to read my letter and, so long as I've written it, I hope a lot of them will. I assure you my publisher will make them pay much more than postage for reading it.

Still, if you could give instructions to your postal employees, I would be happy if they favored certain classes of correspondents and especially if they avoided others.

I have no desire to be read by persons who read with only one eye—whether the left or right, it doesn't matter. I will be annoyed to hear, on the one hand, that this book is a series of pretentious, elementary blasphemies; I will be even more annoyed to hear that Escarpit is becoming a tool of the priests, that he is a changed man, and as a matter of fact "we told you so" a long time ago.

In any case I shall hear from both sides, but not, I trust, too vociferously. Morons depress me. I should also like to hear from those who read with both eyes, who sometimes laugh and sometimes keep quiet—which would lead me to hope that I make them think.

Anyhow, here are my words. Scatter them to the four winds like the dandelion seeds on the cover of the Larousse dictionary. God will recognize his own.

Robert Escarpit

TO GOD

Bordeaux, June 28–July, 1965

You, sir, who are called all-powerful, how is it you have never been able to interest me seriously in the problem of your existence?

Perhaps you have never tried. Perhaps my opinion doesn't matter to you. In which case we are quits.

But I doubt it. If you exist, it is certainly harder for you to ignore my existence than for me to ignore yours. A flea can live quite comfortably without being conscious of the mountain of flesh that nourishes it and eventually will kill it; but not the other way around. To the large animal the insect bite is much more important than death is to the tiny creature.

Let me put it in another way: However infinitesimal I may be in your eyes, you cannot allow yourself to consider me a negligible quantity. First, because I'm a nuisance, a real pest. I sow discord in the little corner of the universe you have so lovingly and—let's be fair—so cleverly arranged. I disobey, I

19

touch everything, I kill, I think, I cheat, I hope against hope, I am so perverse I even try to guess some of your intentions—to oppose them, of course.

All you can do is simply to hustle me back to nothingness by the quickest route when you are in a good mood; or to do so with a few complications and refinements— pretty dull alongside those I can imagine— when you are in a bad mood.

Now that's a rather feeble defense. Your current method—individual killing or wholesale slaughter in varying degree—is not working out. I am reproducing faster than you are killing me. Your efforts are about as effective as mine when I try to get rid of all the mice in my house.

Nor is general extermination any better. You know that; all the history books prove it. On every occasion you have drawn back from the final solution and ultimately preserved the race—thus enabling me to multiply once more. Why? Oh, you don't have to tell me. It's quite understandable. If I were to disappear from your creation, you would never know why the devil (I beg your pardon!) I existed.

True, I don't know why myself, but for a creature who lives from day to day such ignorance is bearable. I can think up temporary aims, working hypotheses that last just as long as I do. But you who by definition are supposed to know everything, if you kill off all human beings something will have escaped you for good. And all during the eternity of your existence you will bear the crushing weight of this unanswered question.

Having said this, believe me, I'm not trying to escape my obligations toward you. Whether I believe in you or not is not crucial; but the fact is I need you, if only as a stopgap.

You who are a perfect, complete, consummate, inviolable being— you don't know what it means to open out to nonexistence at both ends of one's life. A man's life is so full of buffeting winds that it would be unlivable were it not possible to invoke your reassuring presence at the most threatened places. *God be with you, thank God, God forbid, God knows, in the name of God, for God's sake—* you are in my mouth every time the wind from the void blows a little too hard through the slats of my existence.

It is purely metaphorical, mind you, but don't you find this confidence in your name no less moving for all that?

Still, to downgrade you to this subordinate and formal role would be paying you a grudging tribute indeed. You are worth more than that.

One day my friend Merleau-Ponty,* on a visit to Mexico City, noticed the bunting which some liberal arts students had hung on their building in reply to a provocative banner of the law students. "Yes, God exists!" the latter proclaimed. "No, God does not exist!" retorted the former. Whereupon Merleau-Ponty shook his head with a smile and told the humanities students that the only valid reply was rather: "What a pity that God does not exist!"

Thus he went almost half the way toward those believers who like to say: "What a pity if God did not exist!" and then use that as an argument by which they try to convert nonbelievers. The whole difficulty in

---

* Contemporary French philosopher, a noted representative of Existentialism.
[Here and throughout, footnotes are the translator's.]

conversion is in passing from polite regret to retrospective and reassuring fear.

Actually many people think that a world without God is something too sad, too absurd, and too cruel to be possible. And that strikes them as reason enough to believe in you. I have often been told that if one day I were placed in one of those agonizing, unbearable situations in which our human condition sometimes places us—whether as a result of your ingenuity, chance, or some play of forces which neither you nor I suspect—and sought to retain my sanity in life, I would have no other recourse but to believe in you and acknowledge your omnipotence.

Possibly so. Even probably so. But it is just as probable that if I lost a leg by accident and wanted to retain my balance, my only recourse would be to get an artificial leg and lean on it as if it were the real one.

This orthopedic notion of divinity has some merit. I have as much respect for it as for the anesthetic conception, according to which belief in you helps one to die.

But respect is not enough. Sometimes I need you in a different way. In my life I have had occasion to see death rather close at hand

and, based on my limited experience, I think I can imagine what anguish is. When my time comes I have the feeling I shall be able to face up to it alone—badly, but all alone. It is in moments of joy that I miss you. In the midst of joy I suddenly feel sometimes the oppressive weight of an empty sky.

Your religion is much less eloquent about happiness than it is about suffering. I understand why. Since you are perfect, eternal, and immutable, how can you appreciate this grasping at tiny victories, this nibbling at petty pleasures, this snatching at fleeting and fearful delights in our day-to-day hunger for happiness—a happiness that is scented but short-lived like the green wines of the Basque country? You know only the yawning immensity of the beatitudes and, since everything outside you is in disproportion, you see in the human creature only the despair of the fallen god who remembers heaven.

One day when I was in the seventh grade at school, my parents gave me my first fountain pen. It was just what I had dreamed of: in mottled red-and-black ebonite. The gold pen was retractable and its point was reinforced with iridium. I put it where I still keep my fountain pens, in the inside left pocket of my coat. Throughout that first day I felt it against my heart like a captured treasure. When I used it, it was a pen. When it lay in the darkness of my pocket it was a wonderful, extraordinary secret. From time to time I made sure it was still there, with a gesture that was more of a caress than a search; it is a gesture I still make when I have something precious in my pocket or my heart. And each time gratitude welled up in me— what you no doubt would call an act of grace.

Of course I had said "thank you" to my parents. But to whom could I say "thank you" for having parents to thank? Whom could I thank for the custom of giving birthday presents? Or for the spring which, for me alone, invaded that cold, bleak, and grimy Room 2 of my school in Libourne when I touched my fountain pen with the tips of my fingers?

Happiness comes easily to me. What I don't have is someone to thank for it.

You may say to me: "Very well, my dear friend, you don't believe in me and I can understand that it may seem hard for you to express your gratitude to someone whose existence you don't recognize. But am I not present in all my creatures? By addressing one of them you address me. Why not thank the person responsible for your happiness? He or she will forward the message."

Ay, there's the rub. The joys I am given are the ones I like least. I even have a special soft spot for those I steal. True, that kind of stealing doesn't deprive the victim; just the same, it seems a little overdone to offer thanks in cases like that. Did Adam thank you for the apple? And yet . . .

You see, your apples are rather expensive. Our species has paid and paid for the joys that theft brought us. Besides, that's as it should be. I prefer to pay. Thanking is something extra.

I paid for my childhood fountain pen. I'm paying for it this very moment as I scribble on this page. I pay for it in swarming, fleeting thoughts that I strain hard to catch, tame, and then harness to language. I pay for it in intellectual sweat, in troubled thoughts I try to formulate so that I can fight better against them, in moods of anguish whose indefinable traits I attempt to seize and define.

I'm a good payer, at least I try to be. Payment is part of the joy. But the need to say "thank you" remains. When all is said and done, I wonder if I shouldn't address my thanks to myself. After all, my happiness is a thing I am creating for myself. It's quite an art. One is gifted for it or not. I think I am.

Of course, one needs raw material. If somebody has to provide it, why not you? But raw material is raw only because something else comes after it; and I am the one who furnishes this something else. You produce, but I use. You create, but I live. I am the only serious customer for your industry; but I must say, you are not an easy one to do business with. Even though I'm beginning to understand some of your trade secrets, I have no guarantees regarding your delivery time or conditions of payment. That is why I am forced to behave as though you did not exist, to take things as they come, and get from them what I can.

Really, you should be grateful to me for it. One day you said to Charles Péguy*—

* French writer and poet, adherent of Christian socialism; killed in action in the first weeks of World War I.

at least he claimed so—that if I were no longer here, there wouldn't be anyone around to understand the things you do. I say that if I weren't here there wouldn't be anyone around to do all the things you have wanted done.

Then what would you be? Nothing but a figurehead, or one of those writers of immortal fame whose works are encased in shroudlike bindings in the paradise of unread books.

A book is also a raw material. So long as it remains a prisoner in a library, so long as no one opens it, what difference does it make if its pages are white or black, its ideas rich or poor, its vision of the world narrow or inspired, its style noble or vulgar? None of all that has any meaning. They are thoughts in the wind, speculations about non-existences. A book is not here unless a reader is here with it.

It is when I take hold of a book that it begins to exist. It is when I read or when—others having read it—I am caught up in the swirl of their reading that its pages come to life before my eyes, in my thoughts and in my gestures. Then the book becomes real and feeds on me as I feed on it. All I take from it, if it can give it to me, is what I arouse in it here and now. After which it can return to the void.

It is the same with your creation: it exists only when we make use of it. And it does wear out.

Yes, I am a good customer. I don't miss any opportunities or let anything pass. I go through life with wide-open eyes and light-fingered hands. Count on me to empty out everything, from garbage pails to treasures; but don't count on me to draw up an inventory of your wealth and help manage your heritage.

I know . . . People who believe in you behave differently. More power to them! Their eyes are not in the same place as mine. Theirs are inside their head, to help them remember better. Living that way would embarrass me.

I am reminded of that talented lady journalist I once guided through Mexico. Every day I would take her to an adventure with an ornate church, a volcano, or with fellow human beings. And each time she would miss the adventure before her. Looking at it without seeing it, refusing to allow the things around her to come alive, she opened her inner eyes on memories of the previous day and vividly fitted them into the ideal image of a Mexico whose profound soul was thus revealed to her.

I remained at the level of the colors, perfumes, tastes, voices, smiles, tears, and angers. Plato called them shadows. He would have put a dunce cap on me and made me stand in a corner at the rear of his cave. But what does it matter if, from these shadows, I make my scenario of life?

In a cinema the movie buffs remain impassive and ingeniously try to figure out the truth of the story, the setting, the camera work, the editing, and the acting. I let myself go, I laugh, I cry, I get indignant, I grow excited, I enter onto the screen and remake the film alongside the actors, because they are my two-dimensional brothers. I have even been known to applaud an empty screen that conceals nothing but a jumble of ladders, cables, and soiled plaster.

Similarly there are occasions — on a beautiful day lost in your eternity, on an invigorating morning, on a mellow evening, in one of those perfect moments when things fall into place like pieces in a jigsaw puzzle —when a wave of enthusiasm sweeps over me and I get the urge to applaud.

If you find such applause agreeable or useful, accept it without further ado. It is all I can offer you in the way of prayer.

All right, I see you coming. You have the same far-off, quizzical smile as the philosophy professor I had when I was a college freshman. That—oops!—devil of a man would lead me insidiously right into a Socratic trap, stroking his beard with pleasure as I writhed in embarrassment; then he would open an escape hatch with a dialectic that was invariably Christian. You can't imagine how much bad faith I needed to keep from being converted.

Yes, you have the same smile and you think: "I have him. He claims he doesn't know if I exist, but he addresses me, writes to me, talks to me, and, to use his own line of reasoning, even if at the outset of his remarks he could claim I don't exist, now he can't deny my reality since he himself has assumed it by proposing a dialogue. He talks to me, therefore I am."

Hold on now! You are. You're just playing on words. As a Spaniard who had read Sartre said: *No basta con ser, hay que estar.**

* Untranslatable play on words: in Spanish there are two
words for "to be" — *ser* and *estar*.

Don't make believe you didn't understand. Everyone knows you have the gift of tongues.

I talk to you, but I talk to you in my mind. You are; but you are not here, present before me and outside me, taking shape in a body like mine, in a voice, a look, a short-lived, uneasy, demanding life rivaling mine. I know some twenty drugs, a tiny dose of which would make you disappear the way an aspirin tablet rids a drunkard with a hang-over of the little pink elephants he "sees." Nothing proves to me that you are not a little pink elephant in my metaphysical hangover.

Granted, talking to someone does confer a kind of existence on him, but that doesn't imply that he is alive. We also talk to the dead and, to console ourselves, make believe that that enables them to live again. If all the people I speak to daily were alive, I'd never stop beating my brains out or having them beaten out. Let me tell you something confidential, but please don't repeat it: most of my contemporaries are dead but no one has the courage to tell them so.

"He's dead and doesn't know it," my friend San Antonio has written somewhere. Yes, San Antonio. Don't look in your catalogue of saints. This San Antonio has nothing to do with Saint Anthony—except maybe in lechery. He writes wonderful detective stories which the "in" people find terribly vulgar.

You probably haven't read them and, if you have, I imagine you don't like them. From what I know of you, I would say you prefer to read Alain Robbe-Grillet and Jack Kerouac instead. Unless you're the kind of guy who shuts the door of your office in Heaven and secretly relaxes with the Adventures of Superman—then claiming later that the most beautiful songs are the ones that bore us to tears. There are people like that, I swear to you. Besides, for all I know, you may be so broad-minded you frankly enjoy San Antonio as well as Saint John of the Cross, Saint-Simon, Saint-John Perse, Saint-Exupéry, and Sainte-Beuve. But I'm inclined to doubt it. My conception of you doesn't fit in with that kind of reading.

To come right out with it, sir, I suspect you of being a left-wing intellectual.

Oh, meaning no offense, I assure you. I'm not especially right-wing myself and am in a profession that is sometimes considered intellectual. So it ill behooves me to reproach you with belonging to a group with which I am affiliated, even though I am not a typical representative.

You see, a left-wing intellectual is a little like a devil without horns. He is a person who ardently desires the revolution but demands that it be well mannered and revolutionize only what he feels in his mind and heart should be revolutionized. He can be recognized by his noble soul, and his favorite weapon is taking a stand in the form of his signature at the bottom of a well-written statement.

What I am saying, mind you, is not said in mockery. The left-wing intellectual has all the more courage the more he sticks to his ideas. That is all he has more of than other people—and it is a lot. He holds so strongly to his ideas that sometimes he betrays them when circumstances force him to choose between them and the human beings for which they are made. But so long as he does not betray, he is effective. His gentle stubbornness, his nearsighted view of history, defies oppression, shatters tyranny, and ends by causing the temple of the Philistines to crumble on his head. He dies in the process, but he doesn't care. He is sustained by the curious illusion that true life is elsewhere. No doubt you do not find this illusion curious —and for good reason. But I do. I find it all the more curious in that the left-wing intellectual is not necessarily a believer. If he is, well and good, we know what we're dealing with. If he isn't, I imagine he would like to be.

Every left-wing intellectual has a tiny angel slumbering in his heart. Like Hop-o'-my-Thumb he marches with firm step toward the ogre about to devour him but thinks he has saved everything if the pebbles he drops along the way attest to his passage and mark the road that your martyrs, before him, have taken.

"We are idealist Marxists," a friend of mine, a left-wing Polish intellectual, said to me one day. The fact is there are many more priests than Communists in Poland.

I would not be surprised if in Heaven there were many more Communists than priests. If a Congressional committee in the United States looked into your qualifications for entry, I'm not sure the investigation

would clear you. In Spain they tell the following anecdote: after his death General
Franco has a long conversation with you. He
comes away looking worried. Curious, like
all concierges, Saint Peter asks him: "Well,
General, what impression did the Lord make
on you?" Franco replies with a frown: "Oh,
he's not bad, but politically he's not reliable."

In reality I think you have read Karl
Marx and digested him badly. You have that
in common with my friend Lucien Goldmann
who considers himself a Marxist sociologist
and sometimes has enough clarity to admit
he is a theologian.

You and he would agree that the devil
must be a positivist. One can be a positivist
—I lean somewhat in that direction myself
—but one must be so in an intelligent way.
The devil is not intelligent. He has read
Auguste Comte and has digested him badly.
Proceeding from the notion that knowledge
means ability—an idea which, parentheti-
cally, is not so stupid—he tries to make us
believe that dominating the universe means
noting, counting, classifying, decomposing
and recomposing, logically organizing and
causally linking the phenomena by which it

manifests itself. As if one should not be concerned about these phenomena and in any case not make any value judgments about them. The devil is not amoral; he is insipid, colorless, odorless, impassive—in a word, as Camus would say, a stranger. Hell is objectivity. It's a place where one's hands are always clean, one's nose plugged up, and boredom prevails.

For the devil things are as they are. For Marx and for you a thing cannot simply be. It is good or bad, mine or someone else's, here or there, to be taken or left; it has to be or not to be, but it is never satisfied just with being.

At bottom both of you believe—I do oversimplify, don't I?—that nothing that exists can be indifferent to man, that everything concerns him. Along with this common attitude goes a kind of convergence of intentions; among those intentions the most important might be defined—I assume you have read Teilhard de Chardin—as the full realization of the human phenomenon.

Unfortunately it is here that you part company. With a good deal of logic and common sense, Marx places this realization of the

human phenomenon within human beings
themselves. But you pull back from this log-
ical position, fearing it will leave you out of
the game and doom you to uselessness. So
in this creation in which everything is either
this or that, you make an exception for yourself. You alone are the one who is, and it is
in you that everything, including man, is
realized.

It's a neat sleight-of-hand trick. All of
a sudden you are both necessary and un-
touchable. Hats off—or, if you prefer, halo
off—to you! The devil, of course, doesn't
understand that. He goes on teaching us that
divinity consists of knowing good and evil,
not in practicing them, building them, living
them. And when all is said and done it is the
devil who is left out of the game and useless.

No matter how sly he claims to be, you
are slyer; for you have clearly perceived the
double trap of participation and detachment, of commitment and objectivity. The
latter excludes you and makes you nonessen-
tial; the former takes you in and strips you
of your divinity. When you were a very
young god, you used to choose now one, now
the other solution. But when you revealed

yourself in picturesque anthropomorphic guise, the irreverent Greeks plucked your mythological beard. And when you were formidably remote, unpronounceable, and unimaginable, there was always some poet whose only answer to the eternal silence of the Divinity was a cold silence of his own.

Two thousand years ago you hit upon the idea of proclaiming yourself immanent and transcendent at one and the same time. You hid the incompatibility of these two characteristics beneath the veil of sacred mystery. Top secret! *Défense de comprendre! Streng verboten!*

That's what the devil cannot forgive you for. *He* wants to understand. For myself, I don't give a hoot. I'm interested in results, not methods.

The most obvious result is that you remain between two stools. That's why I associate you with a left-wing intellectual. You claim to be both an active fighter and a judge, to wage the struggle for existence together with men and yet you indicate good and evil to them without any reference to that struggle. I don't really see how you're going to manage that; I'm not sure you yourself can see how to do it.

Oh, I don't doubt your ingenuity. The devil may not have any ideas, but you have too many. You know how to handle dialectics —but what is your general line? What's the use of maneuvering if east and west are not on the same compass? How can one hug a coast if he doesn't know what two points he's sailing between? If it's impossible for him to move from one side to the other without changing universes?

In a word, can one get an ideology from a theology?

That is why, in the final analysis, your quizzical smile does not fool me. You can always draw me beyond the horizon by using the chorus of your angels like the sirens' song; you can disrupt my poor compass; but you cannot prevent me from navigating with the naked eye, from living my life on board with the other members of the crew, from deciding together with them the port we want to reach at the end of our brief journey, and from joining my efforts with theirs in keeping the ship from plunging from your infernal Charybdis into your heavenly Scylla.

"Intellectual," you say. "Well and good, but why specifically left-wing? Without mentioning middle-of-the-roaders, there are also outstanding right-wing intellectuals."

True. I even confess that I find right-wing intellectuals more amusing than those on the Left. At least they have a sense of humor. They don't deserve credit for it. Humor is difficult only for honest people. For cheaters it's child's play, since they can see both sides of the cards. According to Bergson, that is what makes us laugh.

Your great white beard quivers with indignation. "Cheater, cheater," you growl, "the word comes easy. And why, Mister Egghead, do you say all right-wing intellectuals are cheaters?"

You're naïve; that's what constitutes your charm. You'll never be suspected of cheating. You are good faith in person—or in three persons, if you prefer. You conceive of cheating only in its elementary form, so to speak. You have no trouble unmasking those who, wishing to play the angel, behave like fools; but you are hoodwinked by those who

43

play the fool in order to win their halo or who play the angel for fear of being fools.

First, I have to teach you to differentiate the Right from the Left. On the Day of Judgment that will save you from disastrous mistakes in screening. Then I hope to be able to convince you to stop considering the Left as the abode of the condemned. That's an absurd prejudice for which you pay more dearly than you think.

To be on the Left means to be humble but not modest. A character says something like that in a play by Sartre entitled—and correctly so—*The Devil and the Good Lord.*

As for lack of modesty, I've already told you what I meant by that. It's the fearlessness of the nearsighted that enables the bearded, bespectacled Davids, fountain pen in hand, to attack the Goliaths of good intentions, or a Zola to write *J'accuse.* It is supreme disdain for status that permits the respectful prostitute to point her gun briefly at Fred, at his father the senator, at his grandfather the governor of Mississippi, at his great-grandfather the friend of George Washington, at the history of the United States, and at all the moral forces in America, and of Americans.

The prostitute deserves even more credit than Zola, because that kind of aggressive effrontery comes more easily to an intellectual who likes being paranoid. As you know, pedagogical paranoia has always been one of the most effective traits in those who have preached your Gospel.

Intellectual humility is harder to cultivate. It consists in regarding the little knowledge and few talents we possess, not as proofs of superiority granting special privileges or conferring special authority, but as weapons to be used for the common good. The occasional possession of such weapons—for a science is so quickly out of date, a mind gets rusty so soon!—creates only responsibilities for us.

I mean real responsibilities, not royal prerogatives camouflaged as responsibilities which that dear old boy scout of a Rudyard Kipling—watch over him!—called "the White Man's burden." Just look at the burden the well-to-do citizen must bear. A heavy burden indeed! It includes all the comforts needed for spiritual beauty, all the law and order required for calm judgment, and a built-in faith in the future that enables him to escape the present moment, make plans, and count on a decent death that may even, without exaggerating, turn out to be noble, heroic, or tragic! And above all it is a burden which buys him the right to choose, give orders, teach, and to lead.

Now look at the other scale of the balance, at a really heavy burden: the carefree "happiness" of the shoemaker, the little man, the muzhik, the worker, the primitive man —good or bad—lapping from the dog bowl whatever he is given. Of course I admit that what he gets is not always so bad or so scanty! The broth of the exploited may include a refrigerator, car, telephone, medical care, the right to vote, and even some education. But dogs are often treated better than human beings because, being dogs, they don't bite when the soup is good.

The free man bites and the intellectual is one of his jaws. Have we really understood the meaning of the weapon Samson used?

Here is where the problem of humility arises. For his mind to function normally the intellectual must have a reasonably full

bowl. It is only with saints—if there are any
—that the voice of the spirit continues to
rule over that of the flesh when the belly is
empty and the fingers numb with cold. But
I don't think that holiness is compatible with
intelligence.

Anyhow, the intellectual isn't content to
lap up the soup: he has to think it, analyze it,
discuss its preparation. That's his way of
tasting—and even digesting. His body may
accept or reject the food; his mind calls it into question. The consumer becomes a con-
noisseur. From his eating experience he de-
velops an ideology or fits this experience into
his ideology. In either case he gives the broth
an esthetic or moral seasoning. Don't ever
scorn this seasoning: A subtle combination
of spices can make a soup tasty or uneatable;
it can make life worth living or horribly dull.
Intelligence and sensitivity are the salt of
the earth. The devil eats a bland diet.

So it is in the soup bowl that betrayals
begin. The betrayal of the Left—ask John
Steinbeck—is to be found in the seasoning.
The betrayal of the Right is in the stew, the
bread-soup, and the dishwater.

To be on the Right means to be neither

humble nor modest. Above all, it means
never to admit it either to oneself or to others. It means belonging to a corporate group
that hides its hankering for world domina-
tion under an ideology that is usually religious, sometimes attractive, and always
brilliant. Don't protest that under those
conditions political thinking in the world has
for centuries been almost exclusively right-
ist. It's a stupid wager that you are bound to
win. To rouse men's consciences the Left has
had to take the road of the body, not the
spirit, for the latter is hampered by too many
illusions and mirages. You're well aware of
that. Long ago you realized that, to talk to
the masses, you had to do so from the cross
on Calvary, not from the professor's ros-
trum. Jesus owes much to Spartacus.

We must bow to the inevitable. Until
recently the intellectual has been a kind of
park attendant thinking up valid reasons to
keep the masses off the lawn—which has
been reserved to his clan, his race, his city,
his caste, his class. Every once in a while a
brief flash of conscience appeared, illuminat-
ing the reasoning of a Greek Sophist, the
teachings of one of your apostles, the anxiety

of a Seneca, or the preaching of a Wycliffe.

I know; it's not your fault. You didn't want it that way. On the cross, when the veil of the future was torn asunder, I imagine your worst suffering was to discover how your attempt to take the human road would be betrayed by the very ones who were supposed to follow it. Terrified by the great upsurge of the masses, they turned into Doctors of the Law and shut the doors of the temple on your grave.

If I know anything about you, your hopes probably quickened again for a time when the Reformation seemed about to beat down the wall and force open the doors. Alas, it was only one class driving out another— a new corporate group forming to defend the interests of the rising bourgeoisie. Protestantism—slaveholding, capitalist, commercial, and industrial Protestantism—was even harsher and more hypocritical than Catholicism. When Molière's *Tartuffe* was translated into English it was given the title *The French Puritan*. I don't know which fills me with more horror: the bonfires of Salem or those of the Inquisition. Perhaps the former, because their flames are still burning in the United States.

Don't think I am trying to defend the purity of your religion against your believers. That's not my affair. But speaking man to man—that's what you wanted, wasn't it?—I can't help complaining to you. If a short while back I took the liberty of referring to our friend Kipling, it was because the two of you have been equally naïve and have experienced the same disappointments. Kipling paid bitterly for his utter faith in the British Empire when he discovered, a little later, that all that love and all those sacrifices simply masked the lust for profit of a money-making machine. Then (you remember: ". . . you'll be a Man, my son!") he uttered this cry that must have awakened many echoes in you:

If you can bear to hear the truth you've spoken
Twisted by knaves to make a trap for fools . . .

Not only for fools, alas! Poor Peter who caught souls in his net without knowing where his catch would be sold!

The right-wing intellectual is the hawker for the slave market. The whole art of his display, all his alluring gifts of gab, cannot hide the fact that he is himself a slave, selling his brothers so as to safeguard his position with the masters. Whether he does so consciously or unconsciously doesn't matter: an intellectual can never use the unconscious as an alibi. It is also useless to point to examples of his asceticism or detachment from the things of this world. The serenity of the ivory tower, the calm of the monk's cell, the peace of the library are forms of comfort for an intellectual. One can also be paid in that kind of currency.

As a general rule intellectuals prefer other ways. Asceticism is a convenient alibi for those who like more devious pleasures: it satisfies the power drive of the intelligent adviser who prefers to pull the strings for a stupid ruler. It's the revenge of the weak but shrewd fellow over the dull-witted brute; the enjoyment of the lazy sophisticate in bringing about weariness in others; the puffed-up complacent conscience of those who, by their privations, think they have reserved in advance a seat at your side and won an option on their holiness. The desire to rise above human nature is often simply a way of despising humans.

For that is really the heart of the matter. Poor Colonel Bigeard* was way off the mark when he spoke of doing what an animal would not do. The ascetic wants to do what a man would not do, and the would-be ascetic who mimics him—the minor penitent, the run-of-the-mill devotee of hair shirts and mortification—wants to do what a man in his social group would not do. All these exercises in formal humility—washing the feet of the poor or living a hermit's life, visiting prisoners in jail or kissing lepers—are double-edged swords, and the two edges are similar. I hope you can differentiate between them. Personally I who, thank God, am not God, see in them chiefly a refusal to mingle with the mass of humanity, to eat at the common table, to live the precarious life and die the inevitable death of mortal man as you sought to do. Even on the cross you could not help

---

* Ultra-rightist paratroop officer, one of the leaders in the attempt to overthrow de Gaulle during the French-Algerian struggle of the 1950's.

displaying the ultimate weakness of the lost child who falters in the face of a lonesome death and an empty sky.

Instead of trying to imitate Jesus, wouldn't it be better if we looked after those he tried to imitate, those he sought to be? I have no hookup with the special line by which believers claim they are in direct communication with you. Your intentions are even more inscrutable to me than to them. But I can't help feeling that the poor slob who dies with a curse, the miner who disavows you as he chokes to death, the hack writer who pours out his last drop of sweat as he dedicates his soul to the devil, are not closer to you than General Saint Ignatius Loyola and his army of spiritual warriors of the spirit. Anyhow they are closer to me.

Well now! Here I am discussing theology—and not very good or very new theology. I'm stopping right now lest they appoint me a cardinal. Let me stick to what I know.

I know intellectuals and I can tell you one thing: when an intellectual voluntarily humbles himself, it is because of lack of humility; because when one humbles oneself, it means that previously he thought quite highly of himself. When one is truly humble, he cannot lower himself; he is already up to his ears in the same mire as the others. In Spanish they say: *metido, comprometido*— once you're in, you're compromised.

That is why the man on the Right has such a ready sense of humor. He has all the detachment required to practice humor. *Suave mari magno*—smoothly he sails over the ocean. ... And he laughs.

Why not laugh with him if one is not implicated in his betrayal and especially if one is its victim? Why not reply to his sneering laugh with a hearty laugh of one's own? One doesn't get so many opportunities to laugh.

Do you laugh? I do, a lot. It's such a good feeling I'll never get used to the idea that laughing may be a right-wing monopoly. It's such an inexpensive luxury, it would be a shame to leave it exclusively to the scoundrels. Besides, laughter has secret virtues of challenge and insight. A man who laughs can't remain a rascal for long; if he does, his anxieties come to the surface and freeze on his lips in a cold sneer of irony. Right-wing intellectuals have mouths shaped like a chicken's ass or a razor stroke.

Take Gilbert K. Chesterton, for example. He was cunning, fiercely Catholic, and anti-Dreyfus; yet he remains one of my favorite writers. He knew how to laugh and how to fight. He liked boxing, cheese, wine, and France—which redeemed him. He detested Puritans. So, like Giraudoux's Oiax, I won't fight against those whose enemies are the same as mine, the sons of Achichaos.

Istanbul, August 11-24, 1965

The other day, at Yalta, I tried out on
an American tourist my remark about the
bonfires of Salem and those of the Inquisition. He was a Good American—a left-wing
intellectual and Jewish.

It is always pleasant to talk about you
with a Jew. One is immediately at one's ease.
For the Jews religion is a family business
operating in a closed economy. A visitor is
received like a guest, not like a piece of sam-
ple merchandise one is trying to sell. To be
sure, the system is a little old-fashioned in
our modern world. From the viewpoint of
sales promotion the Catholic network with
its many branches and a central shipping office or even the Protestant free-delivery service is more effective. It's impossible to hold
back progress; but the good old patriarchal
methods still have their charm.

However that may be, my American
was on the Left. Passionately in favor of
racial integration, he had taken part in a civil
rights march in Alabama and, together with
the other marchers, had suffered insults and
harassment from southern white racists the

whole length of the route. He was proud of his participation, and rightly so, feeling that by his gesture he had done more for his black fellow citizens and the honor of his country than, a few days after our conversation, the Watts rioters in Los Angeles.

I did not disabuse him. Since you gave humanity the example of the road to the cross, the best of them—even Jews and non-believers—have found it the sublimest but also the deadliest of temptations. It's up to you to tell them that the sole aim of your ascent to Calvary was to bring you among men as they are. It's up to you to tell them that Christ's suffering, sacrifice, and death were means through which a god could achieve the human condition that is already theirs. It's up to you to tell them that a man has something better to do than to bend beneath the weight of the cross—and a man named Brother Jean des Entommeures* thought up quite a different way of handling the sacred wood.

You should tell them all that, but I'm

* Character in Rabelais, for whom Gargantua built the Abbey of Thélème.

not sure you yourself are fully convinced of it. Like many left-wing intellectuals, you have an excessive fondness for gestures and symbols.

In any event, my American was certainly in a good position to know that the Salem bonfires are still burning. Yet he was rather irritated by my comment and retorted that in Spain Franco is keeping up the bonfires of the Inquisition.

"Fifteen—love!" you will say, smiling in your beard at seeing me thus put in my place. You forget that Franco, as well as the Ku Klux Klan, claims to be working for your greater glory.

No, you haven't pinned me down, this time either. Oh, I know the embers of the fire are still burning in Spain and there are enough people there ready to blow on them to ignite the same devouring flames as thirty years ago. The Spanish government has just penalized my friend Aranguren and several of his colleagues in ways that are curiously reminiscent of the late Senator McCarthy's witch-hunts. (By the way, where did you dig him up? On your right?)

But whose fault is it? Would there still

be any Franco movement in Spain if there were not a whole range of McCarthyisms in the U.S.A.? Franco at least doesn't claim to be the spiritual leader of the free world and the champion of democracy; or, if he does, no one takes him seriously. Besides, he doesn't have the means to do the job. His candle would have died out a long time ago if Uncle Sam hadn't relit it with his big fat anticommunist cigar crackling with atomic sparks.

Now we're at the heart of the problem. Despite your secret and unavowable debts to Marx's ideas, you are basically anticommunist. Another widely prevalent attitude among the leftist intellectuals.

Undoubtedly you don't have a monopoly on McCarthyism or anticommunism. In my own country, which is a secular republic, the Minister of Education—a well-meaning, simpleminded man who seems ignorant of etymology—has just suspended a teacher who publicly characterized him as a servant of our educational system. The university Left reacted feebly. I must add that the teacher in question was a Communist. In that case...

Nor am I unaware that Opus Dei now

claims to be an inoffensive group of idealists concerned solely with Christian living, allowing its members full freedom of action in secular matters and limiting its influence strictly to the field of religion. But you have never been one to believe in separate areas or compartments. When men seek to carry out your work, even in Latin, they cannot avoid your political directives. All the careful wording in Schema XIII of the Ecumenical Council doesn't change that one iota.

You are anticommunist and I know why. Communism is the first militant movement in history that has dispensed with you. In man's recorded history not a war has been waged or a revolution made other than in one of your names: Jehovah against Belial, Zeus against Poseidon, Teutobochus against Jupiter Capitolinus, Allah against Jesus, the Virgin Mary against Texcalipoca, the Supreme Being against the God of Clotilda. Always, everywhere, the cry has been: *Gott mit uns!* —God with us!—right down to 1917 and beyond. If only that revolution had been made against you, maybe you would have taken it as a kind of homage. But it was made without you; that's what you cannot accept.

If Lenin had been old Papa Combes,* you would have fought him less bitterly. The Great Architect of the Universe or even Reason deified—that's still you disguised in ways you don't like, I admit, but in which you recognize yourself. Lenin made no effort to try to disguise you. In fact, he clearly asserted your role in history, pointing out that for centuries religion has helped the people endure their suffering just as opium helps a sick man endure his pain. But he proposed a medicine that would treat the source, not the symptoms, of the disease. I quite understand why you did not want to collaborate with him, but then don't complain about the consequences. They have been tragic only to the extent that the advocates of your medicine have sought to impose it to the exclusion of any other kind.

All the noise made by your Church of Silence—in Poland one can't hear anybody but her—cannot hide the fact that your priests and worshipers have suffered less in the Communist countries than in other parts

* Emile Combes, prime minister of France (1902–5), known for his anticlericalism and advocacy of secular education.

of the world where they ban and excommuni-
cate one another, and sometimes tear each
other apart within the same faith.

The Christians who shot the Basque
priests in 1937—were they Communists?
The Christians who persecute Negro ministers in the United States and the Union of
South Africa—are they Communists? It's
not necessary to have read Marx, Lenin, or
Mao for religious fanatics to slaughter, mas-
sacre, disembowel, and snipe at one another
in India, Sudan, Vietnam, and Palestine. I
realize that in the heat of revolutions the
grapes of wrath have a bloody taste, but I
have visited all the Socialist countries in
Eastern Europe as they now are; in none of
them did I see any evidence of antireligious
violence. In some of them you are resisting
effectively, in others you have abdicated. But
religious faith has died out by itself; and the
doors of the houses of worship are wide open.
The priests, ministers, and imams stand before those doors and vainly wait for the
faithful to enter.

Perhaps you have had it your own way
for too long. Perhaps it was too easy for you
to retain your hold on the people through

blind enthusiasm, irrational faith, or fanaticism. You had no competitors. Now you have one who is very adept at using those weapons when he has to, but who in addition has the consciousness of a goal to be reached on this earth, a definite line to follow. It promises men nothing they themselves cannot obtain. If you want to beat this rival, if you are capable of it, you'll have to change your habits and make a serious effort to adapt yourself.

Otherwise, keep a tight grip on the Mohammedanism of the Arab nations and Pakistan, the Judaism of Israel, and all the religions of India; maintain their various antagonisms. It's your last chance to dominate a conflict and prevent the peoples in those lands from looking upon you as incapable of getting them to overcome their absurd quarrels.

Believe me, I'm not trying to convert you to communism. I'm not qualified for that and in any case I wouldn't succeed in convincing you. But for the love of your person, for what I and all men owe the millennial dream of your existence, I would like to try to give you your last chance or at least soften the time you have left to live in what for so many centuries you have considered your creation. I say this without irony and from the bottom of my heart.

A displaced person in this universe you love because you have made it what it is, because it is yours even more than mine, and which I am going to take from you because I am the poorest, the most numerous, and the most desperate, you are going to lose everything. And I have nothing to offer you in return except clear-sightedness.

How can you fail to see the role you are being made to play? How can you fail to understand that you are a pretext—in fact, the most obliging pretext of all, since your instinct for self-preservation makes you accept all allies, even the most paradoxical and degrading? Do you realize that they are exploiting your fear of dying?

You have a right to your opinion. Of course you do! Looking at things dispassionately, it is quite understandable why you refuse to support Marxism and even condemn it. Nor can one blame your ministers if they also reflect this antipathy. But your self-appointed saints, your so-called defenders among the respectable laity pay little heed to your opinions. They use your authority and prestige as a cover for their own opinions—that is, basically in defense of their material interests and sometimes even of their self-centered spiritual interests. What they make you fight in communism, as they have made you fight all revolutionary ideas at birth, is what threatens *them*, not what threatens *you*. They may even be fighting what is closest to you in those revolutionary ideas.

Vox populi, vox Dei—the voice of the people is the voice of God. That maxim has never really been taken literally. For the essential thing is to keep you far enough away from the masses so as not to hear the great cries of conscience that sometimes mount from their depths and talk your language. Once, in Jesus' time, you escaped your personal bodyguard and ran toward men. But you were recaptured and the police lines tightened around you.

You never tried to escape again. Even if you did try, it would not help much. The technique of rushing single-handed toward the crowd, of outstretched arms and riveted hands is still practiced with some success by a few leaders of men who studied your ways in olden days and take you as a model. It will disappear with them. Give up the hope of being a god by popular vote. The big things of our time no longer occur on the public squares; the latter have become too small.

Two thousand years after your first attempt to recapture man, he is again eluding you by sheer numbers. During the past few years mankind has altered in scale. It is not merely a question of demography but also one of communications, industrial technology, education—in short, of mutual presence and consciousness. The world is like the stage of a theater in which the lights go up slowly at first, then faster and faster, suddenly disclosing behind the actors in front swelling masses of supernumeraries who were there, though ignored, from the very beginning and among whom the real action is going on.

Do you remember the final lament in Brecht's *Threepenny Opera*, in the original Pabst film version?

For some are in darkness,
And some are in light.

You can see the latter, but the dark
  night
Hides the others forever. . . .

On the screen the horde of beggars faded away, as they had always faded away up to then, on the morning after their uprising— leaving visible in the foreground only the exploiters of their anger.

But now the screen refuses to darken. It is invaded by an irresistible swarm of humanity, lacking even the ugliness of the Court of Miracles. The scene resembles a painting by Breughel or Dubout, in which the devil himself would be hard put to find the faces of the stars.

Are you ready for this new type of staging? I would like to think you are, but frankly I doubt it.

For thousands of years the humanity you have dealt with directly has been nothing but a more or less conscious minority, protecting its newly acquired status by means of taboos and prohibitions of a closed social group, a chosen people, a city, or a caste. The overwhelming majority of mankind, in the lowest strata of societies or in the unexplored places of primitive worlds, was shut out both from human dignity and the divine presence. They possessed neither the ideas nor the language needed to apprehend their own reality and the possibility of a Hereafter. You were able to reach them only indirectly, with stereotyped words and gestures, rituals translating crudely, mechanically, and arbitrarily not their own meager religious experience but that of the conscious minority.

Don't protest. To this day a good part of religion and almost all of what we call art or literature functions in this very way.

When the world suddenly grew too small, when the Roman city died for having sought to expand into a huge empire, when the barbarian hordes swept down in successive waves on your reserved area, when the scale of visible humanity increased from the thousands to the millions, you were able to adapt yourself by sharing infinitely your oneness in Christianity and later by simplifying yourself to an extreme in Mohammedanism—two ways of popularizing, that is, humanizing yourself.

Having risen on the third day, having returned in triumph from your hegira, you survived and even prospered while the world slowly and painfully absorbed that first crisis of growth of the species *Homo sapiens*. But even before it regained its balance, perhaps because it was beginning to regain it, a second crisis broke out fifteen centuries after the first one. It is still with us. Unknown peoples have appeared on the horizon with new stars, obscure masses have risen from the depths of industrial society. In this century we have gone from the million-scale to the billion-scale. The day is not far off when all human beings—having become contemporaries of one another—will be equally impelled to demand their age-old heritage and will have equal weapons—different weapons, yes, but equal weapons—to win their share of it. Having collectively carried out the duty to multiply you imposed on them in Book I, verse 28, of the contract called *Genesis*, they will demand that, for every single individual, you fulfill the obligations you acknowledged in that same article and the one following. What will you do then if you can't even temporarily keep your promise by opening wide the gates of the temple, as in the time of Jesus and Mohammed? What will you do if the temple is too small, its treasure too meager, and if the crowd refuses to enter it?

By nature you have faith in the future, but there are some signs that should alarm you. Don't you find it disturbing that the two largest human populations in the world —half the human race—have almost completely slipped away from you? One is victimized by all kinds of fakery spawned by misery; the other is in the solid grip of an atheist philosophy that has been its religion for thousands of years and in which Marx's influence has apparently adapted itself better than yours. As for the other continents, what will be left of you when Latin America and Black Africa succeed in transforming your Catholicism and Mohammedanism?

In reality, although men still invoke your name, everything important happening in the world could happen without you— everything, except the burnings at the stake.

Yes, there's the *aggiornamento*—the updating of the Catholic Church. Don't think I minimize its importance or misjudge its significance. We shall return to that point shortly if you wish, but right now can't you feel the grim irony in an ecumenical movement that involves only a small portion of the inhabited earth whereas by definition it should embrace the entire world? Despite your cardinals of every skin color, despite the indisputable authority of a John XXIII, Vatican Council II has clearly and harshly demonstrated the minority nature of the once Universal Church. Even if all Christians were to succeed in reforging their unity, even if Christians, Moslems, and Jews were to discover that they worship one and the same god under three names, the lands they inhabit represent merely a fraction of the nations of the earth.

I know what you would like to say—but don't dare because you know what I would answer. Those nations are the influential ones, the famous ones, the ones who set the tone and dictate the law.

To what extent, and for how much longer?

Don't think I say these things lightheartedly. I owe everything to these European, Mediterranean civilizations that have given us Marx and Jesus, Sartre and Mohammed. To them I owe the consciousness of my reasons for living and the vocabulary of my happiness. I am attached to them, one with them, I can't imagine living without them. But that doesn't alter the fact that having been marvelous, miraculous civilizations for millions of human beings, now, confronted by billions, they must change or die. And for a human civilization to change is to die.

Understandably, I can't sit by and coldly contemplate such an outcome, however necessary it may seem to me. But you? Are you so old and hardened that you find it impossible to give up a highly successful but outmoded experiment, in order to attempt another in which your angels may lose some of their wings but in which with a little luck —and you have that—you may be able to survive?

If I were you, I would leave my old, overindulged, and pampered favorites in their twilight if they can't become young again; I would leave them to their bonfires if they know no other way of defending themselves. And I would go elsewhere in search of the eternal adventure.

Please don't make me blush; and don't
tell me I'm such good company you can't do
without me. I realize it's not my own humble
person you find it hard to sacrifice, but the
marvelous religious culture of the West to
which I am attached—for my unhappiness
and yours as well as for our common happiness. Having given you plenty of trouble in
the old days, for centuries now this refined
civilization, with its sublime books, inspired
works, and exalted teachings in which reason
and faith have pursued their dialogue, has
given you pure joys you are loath to give up.

What handsome children you have
there, sir! I understand why Abraham's
knife trembles in your hand. Nor am I suggesting blood sacrifice to you. I simply think
they're children of the rich, unable to accom-
pany you on the dangerous, messy adventure
awaiting you.

They are so clean and pure. From Pas-
cal's *Pensées* to the angelic voices of the Bene-
dictines of Solesmes, from Milton's *Paradise
Lost* and *Regained* to the white cassocks of

the Protestant monks of Taizé, from the English cathedrals—Bibles in stone—to the Dominican chapel at Vence, they form a brilliant procession whose radiance is unsullied by a single spattering of St. Bartholomew blood, whose glory is untarnished by a single puff of acrid smoke from centuries of Papist and anti-Papist burning at the stake. No vile smells, no evil thoughts. Here everything is order and beauty; luxury, calm, and sensual pleasure.

That's just why things have to change. Let me try to explain by giving a modest example . . . from my own life.

One day fifteen years ago while giving a lecture at Casablanca, Edinburgh, or Bilbao —I can't recall which—I suddenly woke up. I roused myself and looked at my audience.

Ah, sir, what a discovery! There they were: the usual quota of old ladies with time on their hands who attend all lectures; the small group of professors breaking the monotony of their academic routine by listening to a colleague's discourse; the front row of VIP's in attendance because in their lofty positions they felt obliged to listen to the most boring things expressed in pedantic French;

the serried ranks of party members bent on applauding the key words and formulas with which they agreed; and the usual crowd of book readers curious to get a look at the visiting foreigner in person.

In a glance I saw them all and I was horrified. Not that I disliked them—far from it. In varying degrees I have felt fondness, affection, and friendship for old ladies, party members, book readers, university colleagues, and even VIP's. They are part of my familiar universe; I move comfortably among them as if I had my old house slippers on. In their own way they are all intelligent, cultured, sensitive, and they know the rules of the game. They are responsive. I know when they are going to laugh and when they are moved; often my own reaction precedes theirs. I play with them or, more accurately, we play together. In our games we experience those subtle pleasures and sophisticated thrills known only to those who have a great deal to say to each other and cannot hold back anything.

That was precisely what horrified me. I saw myself in the company of these nice people enjoying myself like mad and, as I continued my intellectual daily dozen, I said to myself: "No, it can't be. Not for this did your father and grandfather and all your other forebears spend a lifetime of drudgery in sawmill, office, or classroom. Not for this did you spend your youth studying furiously and now, day and night, you slave at your typewriter, your files, your books, or work your brain cells. Not so you can fritter away in parlor games, however agreeable, the scanty treasure so much effort—and not only your own—has put in your noodle. It's not for your pleasure, not even for the pleasure of these good people who are gorged with ideas, books, and sensations. Think instead of those who line up Sundays in front of the English pubs because alcohol fills an empty brain; think of those who feed their starved emotions and undernourished imaginations with bad movies, Sunday-supplement novels, and comic strips because no one takes the trouble to write or supply books for them; think of those who don't even suspect that they have imagination and sensitivity. If you want to sell your goods, these are your customers, even if they don't know it yet."

So I turned my back—or at least one of

my shoulders—on literature and became involved in what I have called the sociology of
literature. I'm doing something more. I am
a bane of existence for publishers and book-
sellers throughout the world; and, since I'm
not the only bane, things are beginning to
stir. Of course, one can hardly see anything
at the surface. But way, way down, where I
have plunged, I have found new games that
are human games. Maybe I'm wrong, but I
feel I'm no longer playing piddling games.

Mind you, it's a big risk. It may make
me lose my intellectual shirt with a little of
my literary epidermis as well. Literature as
we practice it among cultured, well-bred people is not necessarily what my less cultured
and less well-bred friends— no, not *less* cultured, but cultured and well-bred *in a different way*—call literature. I'm not even sure
that literature is what interests them. That's
for them to say, not me. All I can do is help
them become aware of their taste even if at
the outset it is different from mine, and provide them with something other than shoddy
or second-rate stuff.

Golf and *boccie* are two equally worth-
while games. But it would be the height of

absurdity for a golf champion, eager to help his fellow men, to try to interest workers passing the time of day in a slum area by playing *boccie* in a vacant lot, in the fine points of a brassie or a niblick. On the other hand, if he really wants to get interested in *boccie* because he's interested in the players, he will discover hitherto unsuspected qualities in it. By participating in the game and becoming an expert at it, he can give his team some excellent tips: for instance, the technique of pitch-and-run. Familiarity with the springiness of materials can be a big help to him in placing the balls. As he goes along he may even want to form a *boccie* club with its own headquarters, with teams good enough to meet all comers. So the group will acquire new color and prestige. He may even utilize his know-how and reputation to broaden the club's activities: maybe he can get fields as pleasant and attractive as golf courses for the *boccie* clubs, and leisure time for the players to pursue the game.

This will bring him up against a number of problems that have nothing to do either with *boccie* or golf: hours of work and leisure, wages, athletic facilities for low-income neighborhoods, city planning, municipal administration. In short, he will have to think politically and acquire political opinions. In the areas I have just mentioned, politics means making choices based on working hypotheses. And since the *boccie* problem is not a working hypothesis capable of setting the social machine in motion, our man will have to acquire an ideology.

Here is where the difficulties begin. Throwing himself into politics, he will have little time to improve his technique as a *boccie* player or maintain his form as a golf champion. He will have to sacrifice what he once considered essential: a lovely spring morning on the green, the ineffable joy of a hole in one under the admiring gaze of half a dozen silent onlookers, the pleasures of lighthearted banter with friends at the clubhouse bar. All this will give way to painful, obscure first steps along the tortuous roads of politicking. Never completely accepted by the *boccie* players, he will probably be cast out by the golfers, the former mistrusting his earlier friends, the latter disapproving his new cronies. But whatever he gives up, and despite the yearnings that sometimes steal over him at the thought that he could have continued his easygoing country-club life while appeasing his social conscience by advising, teaching, and laying down rules, he will have nothing to regret.

I am a champion at intellectual acrobatics and double talk. I have had my clubs and my temptations. From *L'Express* to *Le Canard Enchaîné*,* from lectures before society ladies to the nit-picking pedantry of university conferences, I have a whole range of refined pleasures. Sometimes I give way to them because I know nothing better, because I feel at home with them, because the society that looked after my education conditioned me for such things. But then tell me why I've never been able to breathe for long in that rarefied air. Tell me why *e medio fonte leporum surgit amari aliquid* (something bitter rises in the midst of this source of pleasures). Tell me why I seek out all these wearying chores, these complications and irritations, all this backbreaking work that sometimes keeps me chained to my desk, and

---

* Two current French weeklies, quite different in approach.

sometimes sends me on interminable journeys. Work that alienates me, absorbs me, consumes me, and even jeopardizes my family's happiness.

I think I know why. Since I woke up with a start during that lecture fifteen years ago, I have never been able to go back to sleep. I have never stopped looking at myself at every moment as if in a mirror. Do you sometimes look at yourself in a mirror? It's very hard to do so without an immediate feeling of disgust, because one is all alone in front of the glass and despite oneself assumes an air of smugness like some plaster saint. To make it bearable one has to see oneself in it along with others and renounce the halo. I would be unable to retain my self-respect if I yielded too often to the temptation of this intellectual complacency which lures me with its logic and its almost irresistible pull. My conscience is not always easy, but I breathe freely; and when on occasion I note that another breakthrough has occurred in the world because a few screwballs like myself have joined to give an extra push to the relentless upsurge of the masses, believe me, I don't regret a thing.

The trouble is that successful *boccie* clubs have a way of behaving like golf clubs. In my field there comes a moment when those who have been nurtured and molded by the Left and have struggled in the darkness to achieve clarity and self-mastery, proceed to harden their values in dogma and deify the symbols of their success. The name for that is clericalism.

I am anticlerical, as you yourself, sir, have occasionally been in the past. You would still be if you had the courage, but—still behaving like a left-wing intellectual who unwittingly reveals himself—you're afraid that that may make you a little old-fashioned. Have no fear: clericalism and its opposite are both doing very nicely, and you are not always on the wrong side of the barricades. I am sure you could very easily have done without state aid for parochial schools, which puts you in a bad light and stores up difficulties for your future. But was it merely a question of clericalism? I see in it rather the stupid selfishness of men of little insight and believers of little faith.

Just as there is a school of the devil, so there is also a clericalism without God. Take a look at *Le Canard Enchaîné* where there is a ban on saying that Roger Peyrefitte is a somewhat dubious character, because in that publication anything that makes the bourgeoisie belch—including what I think—is sacred. Look at *Les Lettres Françaises** which is getting to be more and more like the house organ of a literary church. Look at the Ligue de l'Enseignement to which I gave ten years of my life and a good deal of my heart. It was born of a cultural revolution ushered in by the public libraries founded by Jean Macé. Once upon a time its members broke down the prison gates of the book and opened wide the doors of libraries for all to enter. Now they are devout as parish priests, bowing before the mustiest forms of culture provided they are right-thinking.

God knows—forgive me, sir—all the love and loyalty I have for teachers in the public schools. For a century they have inspired the people with a revolutionary ardor to acquire the means of culture. They have toppled the aristocratic elite and forced the bourgeois elite to give ground. Look at them

* Left-wing literary weekly in Paris, edited by Louis Aragon.

today. They act like bishops in a new hierarchy, trying to press upon the new elite of schoolteachers born of the people the holy doctrine of their church: Outside the teachers' training schools, no salvation.

And so it has always been. Every hard-won truth and liberty secretes an orthodoxy that kills it. Those who founded libraries for all men now see to it that not all books are allowed in them. Those who owe everything to reading assail the movies. Those who saw in the cinema a powerful tool for education forbid their children to watch television lest it pervert them. Those who eat the cake of good literature would like to withhold from those who have nothing the daily bread of the comic strip or Sunday-supplement novel; they even look upon the paperback book as a scandal.

A door has to be open or closed. Personally, I like doors to be open. So when I get a mounting sense of claustrophobia, when clique spirit wins out over team spirit, I have to leave. Taking up the staff of the Wandering Jew, like him poor and lonely, I have to go elsewhere and seek those poorer and lonelier than myself.

Baquio (Vizcaya), September 12-14, 1965

The other day I let myself go and told you some nasty things about a few of my friends. Don't be misled. They are still my friends. In fact, that's why I can talk so frankly about them. I flatter only my enemies.

Besides, my petty personal details don't interest you. You're yawning, you've skipped the last five pages. After all, I'm not the Messiah.

Rest assured, I don't take myself for you. I'm simply trying to make myself understood. If I've taken myself as an example, it's because I'm overfond of metaphors and parables. But it ill behooves you to criticize me for it—isn't that also your pet sin?

Don't tell me, either, that you haven't waited for me to come along to think about all that. Don't hold up to me St. Francis of Assisi, Monsieur Vincent, Abbé Pierre, Dr. Albert Schweitzer, the Salvation Army, and all your competing companies of missionaries.

I cast no doubt on the good intentions of the missionaries, but they are all members of the Christian golf club who are trying to explain the rules of the game and the regulations of their club to people who don't even know what *boccie* is. You know all the risks involved in missionary work and its disappointing results: remember the quarrels about rituals and the priests' failure in the Belgian Congo. As for the other missionaries, they are men of good faith who have tried their best to live with a situation you forced on them and which they wouldn't dream of abandoning.

It looks like they are going to give the worker-priests another chance. To my way of thinking, they are the only ones who have approached the problem from the right end. I don't know if they have any hope of succeeding. Anyhow, the first time they were dropped—it was from your side, not mine. Undoubtedly some among them have been ready to utter the cry you know well, the cry that haunts you so much you have left it in Greek in your Latin liturgy: *Kyrie eleison!* "Lord, have mercy!" Were you afraid they might be understood?

You're the one implicated, not your ministers. When I talk about taking up again the Wandering Jew's staff, I'm talking about you.

The idea is in your head, I'm aware of that. You inspired T. S. Eliot with an excellent poem in which he compares the hippopotamus to the Church. To sing his love the ugly, coarse, massive hippo has only a harsh and raucous voice, whereas the Church—resplendent, triumphant, infallible—sings its love for you in dulcet heavenly harmonies. Yet it's the hippopotamus who will know Heaven.

But on this earth of hippopotamuses will it know joy? Will it even realize that it doesn't know it? If it understands English and owns a volume of T. S. Eliot's poetry, it will have a chance of knowing hope. But since it understands only hippopotamus language and has never seen a book, it will know despair—true despair, the kind that destroys and obliterates consciences, the despair of lost religions you have not deigned to honor with a visit.

There are also human beings who know such despair. Go and see the motion picture *Mondo Cane.* In it are primitive peoples practicing "the cargo cult." Crushed by the white man's technology, stripped of any de-

sire to live, they have built make-believe air-
ports with tree branches in the clearings of
the dense forest. There, beneath the godless
sky, they watch endlessly, waiting to trap the
great magic birds of the sky bearing wealth
they will never possess.

I'm not suggesting that you become an
airplane pilot and land among them in all
your glory. You would frighten them. They
might take you for an American. Nor do I
think you can send them a new Messiah.
They might eat him; and a piece of intestine
is certainly not as attractive an instrument
and symbol of sacrifice as the Cross.

It's not up to me to advise you how to
intervene. I'm not going to teach you your
business. But I do know two things. The first
is that if you don't go down there, you are
lost; for those primitives or others will
quickly find ways of winning their share of
the heritage you promised them, ways much
less agreeable to you and to me. Their numbers multiplying, they will present their demands to Rome, Mecca, Geneva, Jerusalem,
or Salt Lake City. Are you going to answer
them with the atom bomb?

The second thing I know is that if you

go down there you'll have to change so dras-
tically that your age-old believers will no
longer recognize you. Like those penitents
of bygone days who renounced their earthly
goods and abandoned everything, including
their name, setting forth on the roads of the
world barefooted, unrecognizable, anony-
mous, you will have to slough off the old god
and return to a primitive state, then emerge
from it with your new elect. You are not
asked to die this time, but you will not be able
to limit yourself to risking only one of your
three persons, leaving the two others—as of
old—to guard your heavenly throne. Your
commitment must be total; your renunciation total.

Frankly I doubt whether you're able to
do it. You're the prisoner of your successes.
You have made or inspired too many beautiful things to forsake them without an agony
I can only call superdivine.

Now I know what you're going to tell
me. I'm familiar with my left-wing intellectuals. You're going to say to me: "But, my
dear friend, suppose I admit you are right
and agree that I have to make special efforts
on behalf of these primitives. Incidentally

I'm doing a lot more for them than you think. But suppose I agree; does that mean I have to throw all the rest overboard? Can't I do the one thing while retaining the other? Is it necessary to sacrifice the heaped-up treasures of twenty civilizations to enable a new one to be born? Must an act of justice inevitably entail an act of abandonment that would be a crime? And even if it is inevitable, aren't there cases in which the crime is disproportionate to the act of justice?"

Before you know it, we'll be discussing whether it would be legitimate to blow up Notre Dame Cathedral if such an act of wanton destruction were the only way of saving man from hunger or despair.

I would be inclined to answer yes; but that's a false problem and a specious way of putting the question. At the moment a dynamite charge under Notre Dame would be woefully ineffective as a material or moral solution compared to other technical means that may be just as painful but certainly less dramatic.

Besides, to us humans the problem doesn't present itself in quite the same way as it does to you. The precariousness of our existence and our ignorance of the remote future give us a kind of margin for maneuver. I readily acknowledge—in fact, I'm delighted—that the high dam at Aswân can be built *and* the artistic treasures of the Nile Valley saved—on condition, of course, that persons like Comrade Dudintsev* and Monsieur André Malraux, who are rich enough not to live by bread alone, do the work themselves and tax their own wealth for all the means needed to finish the job. On condition that the fellahin of Egypt are not deprived of a single grain of wheat today, a single hour of school instruction tomorrow, or a single moment of pleasure in the rescued art works later.

Of course everyone will say amen to all my conditions, even if they aren't very sure of fulfilling them. But that's not too serious: there is enough uncertainty about human acts so that, with a little zeal and vigilance, their progress can be guided and controlled.

It's not the same with your acts. What you do is irreversible. The consequences are

* Contemporary Soviet novelist, author of *Not by Bread Alone.*

inevitable, although you're the only one who
knows or claims to know the logic of their
connection.

On occasion you have regretted some of
your acts, but it has never been possible for
you to escape their consequences. You have
sometimes regretted the creation of man.
Neither death on the installment plan nor
genocide has—as I've told you—relieved
you of that responsibility. A single one of
your gestures creates a situation that can
only be modified by another gesture that creates a new situation; but something of the
first gesture still remains, even if it is merely
what it has made impossible. Thus your omnipotence, as you wield it, narrows your field
of creative freedom.

From the moment you created man, you
could no longer behave as though man didn't
exist. You destroyed forever the solitude of
the yawning abyss over which your spirit
hovered in the dark—the blinding confrontation of light and darkness sharing the inert
void of the first day and the idyllic peace of
the fifth day, when there was as yet no living
creature in your image.

You have had and still have—I won't

deny it—some good moments with a few carefully chosen ones among us. You love us all with an equal love—except for a few angry gestures and muscular displays of your terrible right arm. But you see, we are many, really very many, and increasing in numbers all the time. We are invading everything, stepping over all the flower beds on earth and trampling the lawns of outer space. With our big boots we are stomping over the shiny floors and costly rugs of the natural harmonies; we are taking apart that famous clock that can't do without a clockmaker. We are ransacking the cupboards of the molecule, poking about into psychosomatic crannies; we're even going into your kitchen and opening the Frigidaire to steal from you your recipes for genetics. You can't live in peace and quiet any more. You no longer feel comfortable at home. Alas, where now is the calm of sacred porticoes, the serenity of cloisters, the silence of holy shrines?

A few thousand of the elect—that was company. A few million—that was a crowd. But I'm alerting you: Suppose now you have to contemplate a few billion—why, that's a giant picnic, a fair, a carnival, paid vacations for everyone.

Several times this past summer I thought of you as I gazed at the crowded beaches. I must confess I felt sorry for you. I'm certainly in favor of paid vacations and I well remember how I laughed in 1936 at the spectacle of the proper bourgeois being driven from their quiet beaches by the swelling tides of vacationing workers. Since then paid vacations have acquired more style, thanks to camping, compact cars, and organized tours. But the flood has not receded. On the contrary, it keeps on rising and breaks against the ocean tide in huge waves of human flesh.

The good bourgeois have bowed to the inevitable, while the bad ones can always solve the problem by traveling to Italy, where one pays to get on the beach.

Personally I prefer to refrain from bathing at the beaches because I too would like to see fewer people on them. A person can't remake himself. I was born at a time and in a country in which the social class to which I belong was and still is able to enjoy the modest luxury of spending a vacation away from crowds. Hence I have acquired habits and tastes that some might call antisocial. But that doesn't matter. I am only human, and during the few short years given me I shall always find, I hope, a way of avoiding the pleasures of special excursion trains without depriving a soul of a minute's sunlight or ocean bathing. But I'm under no illusions that the progress of technology and democracy will one day make available to everyone all the delights of solitary enjoyment on a fairly deserted beach. I once calculated that each European has at his disposal a little less than two centimeters of coastline per individual. Even if they don't all go to the seashore, even if vacations are staggered and the beaches increased and enlarged, the population density will remain incompatible with the comfort I need for my rest. So let's not be childish: I'm not going to try to save what I myself condemn by wishing others happiness.

Of course, selfishness is never at a loss for arguments. In France I know persons who consider themselves humane, liberal, socially minded, even on the Left, who try to maintain and even develop private beaches on the Riviera. They argue that a private beach lends tone to a resort town, attracts well-heeled summer visitors and so, in the long run, profits the local residents.

Doesn't this argument—which is technically correct—remind you of something? It has often been used in your churches, especially in connection with charities. The rich had to have *their* favorite priest so that the poor could also benefit from having *theirs* as well. It has even been used in religious functions themselves. Although different classes of weddings and funerals have begun to disappear, it's not necessarily the best Christians who receive favored treatment at the solemn moments of their life but the richest, the most influential, the most prominent—in short, those most useful to the community.

True, all this is ancient history. Everything has changed during the last ten years. The Catholic Church, which has been the most sharply criticized, is changing its skin; it recognizes its mistakes and is carrying out its updating. What more can one ask?

One thing: When will you begin to carry out yours?

Bordeaux, September 16-25, 1965

It was King Farouk, I think, who said at the height of his power that soon the only kings left in the world, besides himself and the king of England, would be those on playing cards. He forgot the kingdom of Heaven. Now England has a queen, and Farouk, toppled from this throne, is dead, but you are still there, like a fifth hand at a bridge game.

I simply cannot conceive of a one and only god who is not an absolute monarch. In various ages and cultures you have been depicted as a bloody potentate, a somewhat ribald King Pausole,* a Pantocrator in all his glory, an emperor riding at the head of his armies, an enlightened despot, a paternalistic sovereign with a flowing beard, a mad tyrant, a haughty aristocrat, or a crafty political-minded prince. But no matter who the model has been—Louis XIV, Louis XI, or Saint Louis—no one has ever dreamed of making you a President of the Republic.

That's understandable. The monotheist

---

* Sensual, luxury-loving mythical king created by the novelist Pierre Louys.

systems in use nowadays merely reproduce the political structures of the vanished societies that developed them. They all had a supreme leader who guaranteed order and was the source of law. The Greek city-state, which was polytheist, conceived of a law superior to that of the gods. As for Rome, it was ready for you when Caesar came upon the scene.

That is why you cannot get away from the most ancient attributes of omnipotence. They have been yours for centuries out of mind in which men have created you in their image.

Your difficulties began when new forms of power appeared. For instance, you have been unable to adapt to the forms of capitalist society. No one has ever imagined a coupon-clipping god, a merchant god, a steel-magnate god, or a god who is chairman of the board. But those were the very functions under capitalism that represented, if not glory, at least power.

Let's not even talk about Socialist society. You did seem to vacillate between a Stalin style and a Khrushchev style; but you have never claimed to be a party-secretary god or a god who is head of the presidium of the Supreme Soviet.

Two roads remained open to you, but both proved to be dead ends. In the eighteenth century technology offered you the formula of an engineer god, of which Voltaire was so fond; more recently you might have been tempted by the formula of a Führer god. I won't say that the idea has never even entered your head or that you haven't poked more than just a finger into such complicated setups. But you were too shrewd to continue the experiment. You left that to the devil who, less prudent than you and less ill at ease, doesn't care what disguise he wears. Whether it's a military uniform or a democratic business suit, he's the eternal and occasionally winning candidate at putsches and presidential elections.

You, ensconced in your purple robes of a bygone age, champ at the bit: the shared harmony you envisaged between Caesar and yourself no longer makes sense. You have lost your counterpart and your counterweight in this world. Once upon a time the gestures of homage, devotion, and submission directed now toward you and now

toward the earthly sovereign were comple-
mentary. They justified and sustained one
another. Now humans have lost both the
habit and taste for genuflecting in their social life. Still forced to bow in their spiritual
life, they have to dissociate the one kind of
genuflecting from the other, at least as far as
their attitude is concerned. It's a dangerous
and exhausting feat of gymnastics. A person
may be able to hunt two rabbits simultaneously; but it is absolutely impossible to
pursue one of them at full speed while waiting for the other at the stalking ground.

Some of your worshipers thought they
could save everything by making the century
a reserved area, a kind of temporary ghetto
for the living. The material values that pre-
vailed in it were undoubtedly supposed to be
taken seriously, but they were merely the reflection of genuine values, those of the true
life which, as you know, is elsewhere. Their
intentions were unquestionably good, and
philosophical speculation, from the time of
Plato, had no untoward consequences; but
in the nineteenth century the result was
disastrous. The money civilization that em-
barrassed you—rising capitalism was out-

spokenly Voltairean in its attitude—seized on a good thing and legitimized the divorce between heaven and earth. Thus it obtained intellectual comfort and moral security along with a good conscience. Henceforth things of the mind and spirit were on one side, things of the world and of money on the other.

Everything that didn't pay dividends—not only religion but also art, literature, science, love, patriotism—was consecrated and subjected to the purely spiritual law, *your* law. The rest was Caesar's or at least the thing that took Caesar's place: the stock market.

Oh, it was very convenient indeed! No longer any need to pay the artist, saint, or hero, since their values were not of this world. This was the period that gave rise to the outrageous romantic-capitalist swindle according to which a writer is a failure when he seeks material success and expects a fair return for his work. In the name of that same principle, lovers are supposed to live on air and water, defenders of their country are supposed to let themselves get killed for a dollar a day, and holiness is measured by the poverty of the Gospels.

As for the unhappy sinner who sacrifices himself in order to get rich and thus make the wheels of society go round, he can always hallow his money and lower his income taxes by using some of his profits to establish religious, humanitarian, or cultural foundations.

To tell the truth the system is no longer functioning very well. People only pretend they have faith in it. Capitalism itself isn't functioning too well, and when confidence goes even the most stupid person is smart enough not to accept promises alone. The United States Treasury may well print IN GOD WE TRUST on its dollar bills; popular wisdom adds OTHERS PAY CASH. What will you do on the day—and that day is not far off— you too will be asked to pay *cash?* Everyone knows that in your accounting practices, like those we use in France, payments have to be made within a specified time limit.

Many Catholics realized that you were headed for bankruptcy if they continued to accept in your name this dichotomy between you and the world. So they tried to fasten the pieces of your universe together again without sacrificing the needs of a humanity that wants to feel grown up, to your need for absolute power. Confess that you are doing nothing to help them.

How do you expect them to avoid the perils of paternalism when God the Father has to be refitted into the world in which they live?

I'm not going to remind you of the verses of the Lord's Prayer—a very lovely piece, by the way, and you were genuinely inspired (incidentally, by whom?) when you inspired it. But if your will is really to be done on earth as in heaven, then just pull up the ladder that connects them. I realize—no, I don't realize, I concede for the moment, since you say so, that the human will remains free when men carry out your will. Men, maybe, but what about things?

You can be sure we're not going to let you pull all the strings while we keep our arms crossed. So much the worse for your omnipotence. We're the squatters of this world and intend to organize it in our fashion. Blast the landlord!

For a long time we took things as they came because we had no way of seeing them approach. But those days are gone forever. We can't see much farther than the end of our nose, I grant you, but beyond that limit we have learned how to make hypotheses that are better than mere fantasies. Even with regard to our fate, science and technology give us what fashionable folk call favorable prospects or what the less fashionable ones refer to as historical determinism.

Since you never miss an opportunity to emphasize a point that proves your existence (so much so that I wonder if you don't doubt it a little yourself), I'm sure you're going to tell me that all forecasts and estimates based on natural law presuppose a rational universe of which you alone can be the guarantor.

Between ourselves that argument isn't worth a hoot. First, a rational universe— that's saying an awful lot. At most we've discovered a few of your little idiosyncrasies and, without the slightest guarantee that you're not going to change your mind, we're trying to organize them in some kind of coherent way so as to use or soften their effects, as the case may be. As far as I'm concerned, my confidence in your steadfastness is very limited; and I'm always very surprised when something happens as foreseen. Every time I open a door I have a panicky fear of seeing, not the familiar spectacle of furniture and walls, but a little band of horned devils shouting: "April fool!" It goes back to my early childhood: I used to imagine that the aforesaid little devils were building the world around me as I grew only to destroy it after I passed through, like Prince Potemkin building phantom villages for Catherine the Great to drive through. You can't imagine my amazement when in 1946 I discovered that Mexico City really was where the atlases and dictionaries locate it. Yet I had unhesitatingly bought a plane ticket for Mexico City and accepted a lectureship in that unlikely city. Those were hypotheses. There are others, riskier ones.

The validity of our hypotheses is measured by our needs. A person living all his life in a village accepts as a fact that the horizon is a straight line. A person living on our planet Earth accepts as a fact that the sun's rays are straight lines. When I know the needs of someone living in his planetary system, galaxy, or island universe, I'll give you other definitions of a straight line, if by then straight lines are still necessary. The ultimate truth of your intentions matters little to us. What we want to know is what scientific error is indispensable for us to solve our problem of the moment, as Jules Romains showed in his play *Donogoo-Tonka*.

If we succeed some day in getting control of your plant, it will be from within, by climbing from the workman's bench to the engineer's office; and not by studying management theory in some super-Institute of Technology or super-School of Administration. We're not at all sure that such a theory exists, but if it does it's way beyond our living realities at the moment.

In the final analysis, if life is given us by the givers of life, whoever they may be, I think we shall get to know your creation better than you know it yourself, because we will have re-created it atom by atom, second by second, with our hands and brains. It will take more than a single one of us, of course; more than a thousand and more than even a hundred million. But all of us together, from century to century, we shall get there if we coordinate our efforts and pool our knowledge. You will see.

The thing that should worry you most in our era—or reassure you, since your intentions may well coincide with our plans—is "the knowledge explosion." Of course, our computers don't perform miracles—that's the source of their strength. Miracles are part of the tactics of intimidation by which you try to remind us that all knowledge is hypothetical and temporary. But we know that: you're knocking on an open door. We're still primitives, granted, but primitives with a hard skull and a staunch heart. You may be able to impress some of us permanently and all of us for a while, but give up the hope of impressing all of us for all time. That would mean we have too short a memory and too weak a voice to fit deviating phenomena into the network of our observations, reflections, experiences and hypotheses. True, our individual memories are short and our voices weak, but our machines are able to bind the threads that escape us in time as in space. We may not yet be able to weave a net capable of catching a fish of your size, but at least we aren't frightened any more by the enormous hauls we are making. And soon all mankind will be hauling in the nets.

Your miracles have no hold on that collective way of thinking. At best they can sharpen it by revealing where the present weaknesses in the fabric are and which spots need mending; just as an enemy's gunfire reveals to a battle commander the inadequacies of his own disposition of troops.

"All right," you'll say, "I don't deny men's ingeniousness when it's a question of knowing and controlling things, but can they know and control themselves? My friend, are you unaware of the basic difference between the social sciences and the natural sciences? Or are you falling into the diabolical snare of scientism, and claim to be able to explain man by the laws of physics, chemistry, or mechanics?"

You misunderstand me. I don't claim to be able to explain anything at all. But I do think that your differentiation between the sciences of nature and those of man is an obvious trap. I believe that science is one. You're the one using the scientist bias as a device: you let men handle things and you reserve the handling of man for yourself. I'm well acquainted with the reaction of your faithful when efforts are made to help the artist, writer, sociologist, and moralist by using precise methods of enumeration and statistics, including the use of computers. They protest that the human side of things has to be preserved. They mean the divine side, because nothing is more human than numbers and machines.

In reality all the sciences are human. They all converge toward a single goal: man's conquest of everything in his universe he can reach and live with.

The exploration of the field of possibilities by mathematicians is as militant an act as the elaboration of a new economic system. The rudimentary perception of the laws of history by ibn-Khaldun, Giovanni Battista Vico, or Montesquieu was as much a laboratory conquest as the discovery of a new galaxy or a new molecule chain of DNA. It is all interrelated, even if the researchers as individuals are not aware of it. We are fighting on several fronts. The flier doesn't have the same tactics as the foot soldier, the sailor doesn't employ the same tactics as the guerrilla fighter. But we are on the way to achieving a unified command, and if we don't succeed in absorbing all the data of the struggle, our machines will do it for us.

Between Bordeaux and Geneva, September
27-28, 1965

The distinguished-looking gentleman sitting opposite me reading *L'Express* looks a little like Jean-Jacques Servan-Schreiber,* with a bit of General de Gaulle in the way he holds his head and something of François Mauriac in his glance. Next to him on the seat I see *Le Figaro*, the *New York Times*, and the *Times* of London.

No doubt about it—it's you. I would recognize you among a thousand others. Since we left Libourne I have been silently questioning you. Now as we approach Poitiers I hear you suddenly answering me in my head.

"And what about moral values, my friend? What do you do about them? A while ago you revealed to me a plan for man's military conquest of the universe. You're welcome to the advantages. Conquer, my dear fellow, and more power to you! The role of master of the universe is not an easy one; I

---

* Widely read, contemporary French journalist.

hope you feel happy in it. But don't think you'll be able to do without moral values. I realize that all knowledge is ultimately applied knowledge and all research arises from a desire for action. There is an unbroken chain from Einstein's theories to atomic terror, as there is from Pasteur's microscope to overpopulation and the famines that are the bitter fruits of hygiene. In this sense I grant you that in the eyes of morality science is one. But that is precisely why morality is needed. The examples I have just given you show a science without conscience can destroy bodies as well as souls. But who can be this conscience? Who can establish these moral values—if not me? Will you deny the testimony of Bertrand Russell? In one of his books he openly endorses the position of the clear-sighted cardinal who persuaded Galileo to keep to himself the secret of the earth's rotation around the sun because premature publication of it would have cast doubt on the teachings of the Holy Scriptures, which in that day and age was the only standard of moral values."

There you are! That's you to a *T*. We have a confession—*habemus reum confiten-*

tem. Your rule is based on a pious lie. We'll come back to your claim about establishing moral values. For the moment let's analyze your method. It's exactly the opposite of ours. Our temporary truths are ways of organizing the ground we have covered; yours are ways of giving up ground with the least possible expense.

It's neither honest nor profitable. In the long run you get all tangled up in your repeated lies and when the moment comes to say you have lied, you cut a sorry figure. After all, lying is a big sin. And it's far from easy to reconcile with the profession of morality maker—isn't it?

Oh, you've given the Church leaders at Vatican Council II a complicated job indeed! If from the very first day your revelation had been frank and overpowering, if there had not been a few hundred or thousand Galileo cases since you began to dole out revelations as if with an eyedropper, the unhappy bishops would not now have to wrestle with the insoluble problem of acknowledging the Church's past mistakes—mistakes on its part, frauds on yours—while striving stoutly to maintain the principle of your

116

moral authority.

You have never treated us like grown-ups. Maybe we aren't grownups (to tell the truth, I hope so), but that's no reason for you to leave a little white square permanently blank on your television screen.* Even if we are only children in your eyes, education has progressed in recent years, and family relations are no longer what they were in the days of the patriarchs. Be our father if that amuses you, but at least treat us as we treat our children. Thank God—or rather, thank man—we no longer say amen in modern families.

I'm talking from experience. A father never has much authority over his children; and the day eventually comes when the violent Oedipus conflict has to be played out symbolically. But things go much more easily if there aren't too many lies to clear up.

I am told that the theologians are now going to take up psychoanalysis. It's high time. Do you realize what traumas your preference for fatherly omnipotence inflicted

* The little white square appearing on French TV screens means not fit for children.

on our subconscious when we discovered that storks don't deliver babies, that Santa Claus has a false beard, and that the truth of the catechism has nothing to do with that of the countinghouse?

Clearly, your case is amenable to psychoanalysis. What's more, you know it. You have read Freud, but as in the case of Marx, you have digested him badly. Your trinity is no great mystery and it no longer intrigues me since I have understood its origins. "In the name of Ego, the Id, and the Superego, so be it." It's as clear as daylight.

The darkness hovering over the abyss when you opened your eyes—what does it hide? Relax. Let the original darkness come back over you, let yourself be carried away by it. Doesn't any dream or image rise up from the depths? A mother's face, for instance.

A mother's face. That means something to you. Of course it does. There hasn't been a single religion which, groping toward you, hasn't found one on its path. The face has been severe or tender, tortured or calm, but always virginal. Against what aggression does this desperate demand for prenatal purity protect you? What unavowed nightmare

119

lies behind the moving mask of the virgin mother?

Who was your mother, God? Was she, as Sir James Frazer asserted, a monster of the night peopling men's sleep with fears of death? Was she one of those goddess mothers bursting with energy and vitality who devoured the males and bore the harvests in the pre-Hellenic cities? Was she a Kali with the thousand hands of a strangler? Was she an Aphrodite sated with sensuality and consumed by poisons? Was she an Antinea?

In man's memory there are faint reminders of matriarchal religions that disappeared with the advent of the one god. Your religions, even Christianity, are invariably misogynist. Despite the temptations of the cult of Mary to which your faithful return for nostalgia's sake, you have not made Mary a member of your trinity. You are a male, nor is there any doubt about the sex of your angels.

The Virgin possesses only a reflection of divine power. Her role is to intercede, to plead, to redeem the original sin—which was a woman's sin. Mary's grace assumes Eve's guilt and prevents us from forgetting it.

Woman and guilt—those are the two inseparable themes of your conscious thought. Admit there's something wrong there.

In your eyes every religious attitude is first of all an attitude of guilt. Prayer begins with purification. In your Church no one is allowed who hasn't been cleansed, by baptism, of a sin he hasn't committed. Of course in our daily lives we all make mistakes in behavior for which we can and should feel ourselves responsible—but as human beings what can we be collectively responsible for? An age that condemns collective responsibility cannot allow the stigma of original sin to extend to the whole human species and carry over from generation to generation.

Besides, those original sins seem quite suspicious. One needn't be a detective to spot them as clumsy provocations. Many good minds have begun to ask whether Judas was —voluntarily or not—your victim rather than your informer. As for the business of the apple, you should have planted your tree elsewhere or not have created Adam in your image. In that situation, forbidding him to eat the apple was tantamount to encouraging him to—any schoolteacher will tell you that.

It wasn't the devil who tempted our progenitor, it was you who tempted the devil.

Don't think I'm trying stupidly to deride your mythology. Replace the apple by what it means and my argument still stands. If you wanted man to remain in a state of innocence, you shouldn't have awakened in him the ambition to leave that state or put within his reach the means for doing so. To stir up temptation deliberately is very typical of your way. It almost seems as if you get pleasure in making us feel guilty. Then you expect us to behave like the kid in the nursery school who, facing the stern-eyed teacher, bawls, "It wasn't me, Ma'am! I didn't do it on purpose, Ma'am! I won't do it again!" even when he hasn't done anything at all.

For some two thousand years now you have decided to save us and give us a chance to redeem our sin. It's very decent of you, but save us from what? And redeem what sin? It's very good that we love you; no one will complain about it. But do you have to provoke situations for us to show you our love, by creating in us a kind of juvenile-delinquent mentality?

My friend Roger Nordmann, who is Jewish and comes from Fribourg, a publicity man who supports many worthy causes, has asked me to give you a message. His message is that he did not kill Jesus Christ. It's not that he's incapable of killing someone—but if he killed, it would never be Jesus, not even at the wheel of his high-powered red Triumph. Nordmann is absolutely sure of that. So he thanks you for having prompted his exoneration by the Church fathers at the Ecumenical Council. But he points out that no one was bringing up that old story any more —Hitler's resentments against the Jews were of a different kind. This reopening of the case, however well intentioned, risks putting Nordmann in a bad light and may harm his business. He asks that in the future you consult with people before granting them an acquittal.

Believe me, you've got to give up this kind of behavior. If it's too much for you and you can't check the excesses inspired by your love for us, consult a competent psychoanalyst. You're probably experiencing a transference to humanity. What's more, I advise you to get a doctor who measures up to the patient. If you took it into your head to make a lateral transference, I wouldn't want to be in that unfortunate's shoes! You'd need Freud in person, if you know where to retrieve him in your Beyond.

Maybe he will succeed in discovering what frustrations you are suffering from. That's a risk we have to run. There is no law that says that, once you're rid of your neurosis, the plaything of creation will still interest you. Depending on what you do then, either we shall be truly free, or else it will be as if we had never existed.

That's not serious, as I've already told you. What is serious is that we do exist and are your plaything. The role of favorite doll is really the most unpleasant role imaginable. Little girls love to lecture their dolls and spank them, so then they can forgive them and thus prove their love.

For a god at your age to be playing with dolls is disturbing. Yet isn't that just what you're doing? God, have you ever been a child? Oh, I know, during your human experience, you were a newborn babe, a bambino, a lovely infant Jesus. Later, much later, you were a man of thirty whose charm and authority are still impressive despite the obscure and conflicting testimony about you. But between those two periods? Were you ever a nasty little brat, a brawling snotnose, a restless, pimply faced adolescent, a petty pilferer, a girl ogler, an angry young man, an obnoxious show-off? The Bible is curiously silent about that portion of your life on earth. Was it a case of repression, or did you simply skip that stage in human existence as dull and futile?

If you did, you were wrong. It is during that turbulent period that we serve our apprenticeship as human beings and develop our true moral values.

Your morality reminds one of a policeman and a spinner of fairy tales. It hasn't got beyond the stage of scarecrows and sugar candy. It has remained infantile. On the one hand it says, "Do this, don't do that, or look out!" On the other hand, "Probe your conscience, a treasure is hidden within it."

What do we care about this carrot-or-club game? What concerns us is the marvelous adventure of living. Our law is, first of all, to take possession of ourselves and of the freedom we feel in our bones, our nerves, in every one of our fibers. A man's life has to be altered like a suit, forged like an instrument, refined like a muscle. It meshes like a stubborn, complicated machine. Childhood and youth are harsh ordeals; those who have only rosy memories of them don't deserve to live happily.

First of all, we learn to say no. That's the rock on which all morality rests. Plants don't say no; they die. It's their only way of showing disagreement. A several-month-old baby already knows how to say no and survive. By its refusal it secures its hold on life. It disturbs the natural order so as to find its place in it; it learns of its sole existence among the confused welter of all other things.

Next, we vacillate between yeses and noes; wake up little by little to doubt; feel within ourselves the rising torment or exaltation of doing this or that; try a thousand times before we control this machinery of an open or shut door; learn to steer the torment of our inner contradictions in the direction of a what we feel to be a free choice. Animals don't hesitate; when two series of conditioned reflexes in them contradict each other, they can only groan or die, like Buridan's ass.*

At the same time we build the world around ourselves and do not let ourselves be molded by it. We attack, experience, probe, recognize other freedoms and denials. We avoid the trap of the sharpest gradients and the zones of least resistance. We develop a hard shell against men and things, but at the same time organize them, incorporate them into experience as the latter grows more coherent. We wander about and get stuck in the swamps of this world, but at the same time set up some mileposts and trace some paths in them. At length we locate the position we occupy and the direction we are moving in.

Then step by step we separate light from darkness, striving to see clearly within and outside ourselves. Now comes the moment to overcome the insidious cowardice of our own conscience, that would end the wearisome journey of exploration right there and build a refuge of calm and certitude. It

* A famous philosophical dilemma, discussed extensively by the medieval Schoolmen.

is also the moment to unmask the false freedoms and false constraints by which the conspiracy of the Establishment—one's own and that of other men—seeks to lure one toward inglorious revolts or slavish security.

Finally one day, the latest day possible, having come to the end of our courage and resistance, we reach the age of adulthood, when one has to be what one is. You once said there is a time for gathering stones together and a time for casting them away. Quite right! Unfortunately, when our stones are gathered, we have a tendency to behave like misers and no longer feel like casting them away. That's why we need a morality born of our wrestling with life—a morality that forces us to continue to live even when we have exhausted the aggressive impulses of our youth.

I told you that most of my contemporaries are dead and don't know it. Their pile of stones, whether it's a tiny mound or a mountain, has become an insurmountable obstacle to them. At the top they have planted the flag of their sorry victory and made it the citadel of their pitiable success. Those who have been unable to gather up stones take a heap of rubbish—medals of honor, skin color, unctuous virtue—and shout like the others that they have built a monument more lasting than bronze. Or they try to steal some of the stones around them. Or, in a futile and absurd revolt, they attempt to destroy their neighbor's pile. Or else they despair.

I have criticized you enough not to have to hide our weaknesses from you. Besides, you know them. *We* are not gods. We have to live and die in contradiction, uncertainty, uneasy conscience, fear. Is it any wonder then if weariness overtakes us and we yield to the temptation of falling asleep in the shelter of our ridiculous little mounds? The true moral law is the one that makes us leap out of our shelters like startled rabbits.

Do you think they can succeed—the far-off mirage of your kingdom or the obscure menace of everlasting death you promise the damned? Those are children's dreams and nightmares; at best, they can arouse sleep-walkers and hurl them into adventures they are powerless to control.

But we have to get up in broad daylight and under our own power. What does it matter if the bulk of humanity, sheltered behind the enormous accumulation of its works, is still sleeping? Crumbling under its own weight, this huge mass will soon awaken. Nor is it ever altogether asleep. There are always enough human beings who know the difficult art of systematically destroying the pile of stones after having built it. But there are many, too, who manage to build it up again a little further along the way. I don't know if I'm among them. Alas, from time to time I feel within me the irresistible temptation to be, to endure. I'm making a book out of this letter I'm writing you, and in every book there is the snare of permanence. But I do strive, with all my strength and all my will, to surpass myself. If I cannot live out my span in the transient and temporary, if one day I tell time to stop because the moment is too horrible or too beautiful, then let others step over my body, overturn my proud molehill, and march forward.

Since I last wrote to you, I heard Pope Paul VI's speech at the United Nations. It was more than a speech; it was the act of a clear-sighted, courageous man. I stress the phrase: the act of a man. While he was speaking, the Pope certainly thought he was inspired by you and felt he was merely your spokesman. You and I are less sure of that, aren't we?

Sometimes I ask myself if you deserve the Church that is trying to come to birth in our time. I wonder if, once its difficult period of gestation is over, it may not discover that it's an orphan.

In any case, the other day in New York for the first time in world history a religious leader addressed almost the entire population on earth, including the absent one-third. Don't you find it odd, even disturbing, that he was listened to and was able to move his listeners' hearts if not rouse their spirits without ever referring to you except in his very last words—the way a producer is finally mentioned in a list of movie credits?

As a matter of fact, you may have been

the producer. But the director was a mortal man, neither more nor less. The person we listened to was neither your vicar nor your viceroy but a man named Paul, by profession Pope in Rome.

It was as such and only as such that he could effectively preach morality to us. He brought nothing from outside: neither revelation, promise, nor threat. Everything he told the nations came from the nations themselves. He confronted them with their own image as they have shaped it, naïvely or knowingly, since World War II. I've already told you that if a person has a minimum of insight, no good conscience can resist that kind of mirror. But does one ever have enough insight?

I don't know whether what the Pope did will have any effect. I tend to doubt it. We need more than one speech to blast the boulders blocking the road to peace.

A little later the Pope said mass at Yankee Stadium before the most pharisaical and the most movie-loving people on earth. Why didn't he use the reflective power of his words to show the Americans their own Christianity in the mirror of truth? No doubt he didn't want to mar your triumph and upset your superproduction in Technicolor. Oh yes, I'm sure you were in on it. You're the best ham actor around.

Maybe too he didn't want to deprive the Americans of a favorite toy and plunge them into despair, which is the father of all crimes. Nowadays in the United States, the Christian and specifically the Catholic religion is one of the playthings that sometimes succeeds in dispelling the nightly fears of that spoiled and childish people. Or at least it softens the effects of their contradictory reflexes—their racism, violence, chauvinism, and sense of mission. The Americans are a combination of unhappy child, rich man's son, and Boy Scout grown older. Their despair may lead to the most fearful things.

Despair ... do you really know, sir, what despair is? I mean the despair of a child watching his red balloon float away, or that of an Orpheus who has lost his Eurydice. Against that kind of despair your theological hope is powerless.

It is not the metaphysical despair born of man's disproportion; it is the other face of our good fortune on earth, our fleeting and uncertain achievements. It is the price we pay for them. It is unavoidable, since everything we grasp slips out of our hands from one day to the next, and at the end of every joy comes a moment in which we must lose everything.

What do I care about another life if I can't keep the one that is mine? What do I care about your existence, if you can't give me back what I have lost and shall lose? What do I care if you promise me, humble in spirit, the kingdom of heaven—if I can't have that red balloon today, if I can't love this woman now as people love on earth?

Translate your hope into plain language and you'll see that all the consolation it brings sounds like the bromide: "Lose one joy—and find ten million others"; or: "Don't cry, baby, if you're very good I'll buy you a blessing which, like your halo, will be in stainless steel and guaranteed for eternity." It's the attitude of a children's nanny, slightly senile, toward her underdeveloped charges.

Everything in our life is irreversible, inexorable. What is lost is never found again, for one can never relive the moment that brought, or might have brought, joy. Even if by some miracle you were to reverse time's flow, the refound moment would no longer be lived for the first time; and, in any case, it would be followed by a letdown. Reread the poet Lamartine's *Le Lac*. Isn't that about what Elvire and the poet himself say in the poem?

> *O lac, l'année à peine a fini sa carrière...*
> [O lake, the year has barely ended...]

Remember the fountain pen my parents gave me that October in my seventh year of school? I lost it the following October. Perhaps it was on October 13, like today. And like today the sky over the Gironde River was a golden blue, a sign of a good vintage, of pigeons passing over the hills, of edible fungi swarming beneath the oak trees. I became aware of my loss as I left my Latin class around eleven in the morning. Suddenly the sky pressed down upon me like a leaden weight, the light became blinding and black, the world turned into a horrible machine that causes pain.

Sir, if you know where my fountain pen

is, if St. Peter is waiting for me on the threshold of Heaven to give it back to me with a kindly smile, keep it. I don't want it. I wanted it thirty-five years ago, on October 13 at eleven o'clock in the morning, at my school in the town of Libourne. You may give me back something like the shining substance of my fountain pen, but you will not give me back the moment when for the last time I fondled it in my pocket, with everything that brought that moment into existence, with everything that gave it appearance, thickness, duration, including the cat-whiskered mustache and angular skull of Monsieur Plazol, our Latin teacher, including the one-legged concierge who used to beat the drum when our classes ended, including the game of pelota I was going to play against the wall of the butcher shop when I got home, including the wobbly tooth I was pressing with the tip of my tongue.

My parents were surprised at the sullen way in which I accepted their offer of another pen to make up for my loss. Yet that sullenness was most helpful to me. I still exhibit it when I feel the skies close in on me and I see the sunlight switch to darkness.

When one or another of my family tries to fix things up in a way that will spare me an access of disappointment or depression, I get enraged. It's a stupid but liberating kind of anger. I don't want them to conceal the irreparable from me. It's *that* I hate, it's *that* I want to face up to, it's toward *that* my anger is directed. If it rebounds on the gesture that's meant to help me, it's certainly not because of the good intentions in the gesture, but because of the resignation involved in accepting such aid.

The day my father died, anger overcame grief. Death makes me feel angry rather than fearful or crushed. That evening I was in no mood to hear words of condolence. Instead of that, our family doctor, an old friend, said to me almost jovially, "I closed the eyes of your grandfather and those of your father. Now I'm at your service." Immediately I felt relieved, assuaged by a wave of anger that swept over me at the cold image of a cruel and absurd death. The mirror of friendship doesn't lie.

Yes, anger is the only serious antidote to despair. That's why it mustn't be abused. I dislike anarchists, angry young men, and professional rebels because they burn up in useless fireworks the good powder in our allotted arsenal.

One cannot live in anger. Nor is everyone gifted for anger, any more than they are for happiness. For the moment the overwhelming majority of human beings have only the choice between illusion and despair. Sweeping reforms or a revolution in social institutions, the development of hitherto unknown techniques and widespread education will be needed before we reach the moment when all, or almost all, of us are able to face the pitiless clarity of the mirror.

Meanwhile those who can bear to look into the mirror for a time, until crushed by an unforeseeable catastrophe, have a triple and a contradictory duty. First, they must fit their life to the demanding moral law that rules their inner world but cannot emerge from it; for one should never demand of others what one demands of oneself. Next, they must maintain their clear-sighted pressure on others by denouncing undertakings of the collective conscience and by refusing, insofar as possible, to take part in their demonstrations—which assumes that they are fulfilling their civic obligations completely, and even beyond the line of duty. Finally and above all, they must respect the weaknesses of others and avoid plunging their fellow men into despair. For one day they will discover this weakness in themselves and know personal despair. There is a pride in moral courage that is a form of cowardice.

We must not throw stones at the person who can't bear to see his stronghold against the absurd crumble and who, feeling himself incapable of building another, defends the one he has even to the point of the ridiculous and hateful. We can't refuse others what we must try to refuse ourselves for as long as possible: the consoling illusion which gives meaning—or absurdity, if you will!—to life. The soldier who justifies a criminal war because thousands or millions of his people have died in it, the little white man who fights against poverty and insecurity by succumbing to racism, the semieducated who would like to shut the doors of the schools because his own meager culture is his sole victory over the general mediocrity—they are wrong. Of course they are. But can we take away from them their reason for living without giving them another, without offering them a more fruitful way of averting despair? And can we offer them that without calling into question our whole society, with all its laws and institutions?

There is no collective morality without political commitment. Paul VI traveled only half the road. Nor do I reproach him for that. The Church has never been very successful in politics. But you, Monsieur President-God, if you really want to preach morality to us, it's time you presented us with choices. You've got to formulate your program and take sides before running as a candidate in the universal elections.

And let me warn you: in politics implicit confidence, blind loyalty, the cult of personality may succeed for a few years, so long as men are not too numerous, are exhausted by the aftermath of wars, lack talented figures, and are overburdened with chores. But, believe me, that state of affairs only lasts for a while.

It's nearly a week since I've written to you. The reason is that I've been tied up with the reopening of the fall term at my university. I'm taking advantage of a trip to Paris to resume my letter. Our contacts, sir, occur in motion and on railway trains. I like that. Seated in the train, I have time to think of you and the devil—particularly the devil— when the seat opposite me is empty and I fill it with ghosts.

Besides, I didn't forsake you completely this past week since I spent most of the time preparing my course on Hell in literature. Last year, when we were discussing the forthcoming curriculum on our faculty committee, I commented to a female colleague who proposed this theme that Heaven would have been a pleasanter topic.

"Pleasanter maybe," she replied with a glint of malice in her eyes, "but much less amusing!"

How right she was! You have no literary sense. You didn't invent the Hell of horned devils and fiery furnaces; it was the imagination of men working on the four or five obscure lines you made St. Matthew write in his Gospel. Recently I saw many of Dante's manuscripts, and it is obvious that those few words inspired the illustrators much more than did your long descriptions of the Garden of Eden or the Heavenly Jerusalem.

And do you know why men gave themselves a Hell in spite of you? Why they saddled themselves with nightmarish tortures which you obviously didn't even think of?

I'll tell you why. Because they were afraid of getting bored. Dante's Hell or that of François Villon's mother was the medieval form of tourism, space exploration, and spelunking. It was the spice—an exotic and dangerous spice—deliberately added to the tasteless, colorless broth of eternal death.

Look at the Hades of the Greeks, the Sheol of the Hebrews—endless landscapes of gray, in which the shades of the unconsolable dead wander aimlessly around. That's what we're afraid of. The fear of dying is the fear of surviving without life, without struggle, without pain. What a relief if we could be sure that death was an everlasting sleep and not a surly, everlasting sleeplessness.

You did a poor job when you tried to arrange things by hinting that beyond the Beyond there was a wondrous Paradise that would console us for everything. It's the story of the replacement for my fountain pen, all over again. Secretly men have always rejected your consolation prize in favor of the Hell they have imagined as one imagines one's own movies. Happy Hell which promises us that after death the things we know will continue—even though those things may be judges, policemen, jails, concentration camps, and Nazi SS torturers! A man can stand up to all that, can prove himself by rebellion, anger, hate; and if he has to yield to punishment, the punishment still gives him a claim to the life that earned it.

Since I wrote the preceding lines, I have again been interrupted for a whole week by tasks which I may discuss with you some day. Robert Sabatier, my editor, has paid me a visit. I asked him if I couldn't finish my letter at this point. It seems not; I haven't used up my paper quota.

It is true I still have lots of things to tell you. If you would hear me out like King Schahriah listened to Scheherazade, you'd be forced to forgive me for all eternity. But the fact is that when life tightens its web about me like a poorly dyed Nessus shirt, when I am dragged back to work like an addict to his drug, I think of you less and have trouble finding you again at the tip of my pen. I told you that you were probably a little pink elephant born of my metaphysical hangover. When I work, I no longer have a hangover; I am drunk, and you go where all little pink elephants go. There is no room for you in an ink drinker's, word chewer's, idea smoker's paradise—an artificial paradise no doubt, but a paradise nonetheless. Hell is vacation time.

I like vacations during my working year. It's when I'm on a vacation that it oppresses me. Of course I get carried away occasionally by a vacation and believe momentarily that this letting go is a way of finding myself again. Then suddenly, in a secluded forest, beneath a blue sky, in the midst of happiness, panic grips me. I discover that I am an insomniac, half-dead, a sleep-walker, a pale shadow in a twilight that is fast fading. And I am afraid of that Hell.

I visualize Hell not at the moment in which one sees one's death, but at the moment in which one sees one's life.

When I was ten, I asked my astonished teacher, "Sir, why do I exist?" Luckily, I didn't have a priest handy to address my question to, because the priest would have given me an answer. At first my teacher merely laughed, but then he abruptly stopped laughing as he wiped his eyeglasses and looked within himself.

I know now that my question can only be put to the past. The answer, if there is an answer, has lost almost all its usefulness for living but may help one to die.

Unfortunately there is no answer. The treasures of life suddenly slip through one's fingers when one stops to count them. That's why one must not stop. Life is a Eurydice whom Hell snatches back from anyone who turns around and gazes at her.

If I had been Orpheus, by God . . . no, I'd shock you if I told you what the Gascon in me would have done to Eurydice. I too would have lost her in the end, but I would have lost her as mine.

In actu mori. To die in the midst of action. The crucial thing is not to stop, not to pause for breathing spells. One must devour life, not taste it gingerly. As soon as one stops having a full mouth, it leaves a taste of ashes. Dilettantes are impostors.

It's the succession of gestures, words, and ideas that makes up the moving richness of life. Let me refer to the movies again: try to stop a single frame in a sequence of great beauty and emotion. The result is a blurred image, a frozen caricature like the corpse of a soldier cut down in the midst of his charge.

For life to hold together it has to go from frame to frame. Look here, I've often thought that if I were you and had to invent the most horrible of Hells, I wouldn't change a thing after death. I would merely suppress time, interrupt the flow of events. Imagine the nightmare: suddenly we grow aware of our entire life, from one end to the other, as of a single, completed, unchanging object, an island in the infinite; we would have *simultaneously* in our hands everything we have touched, in our mouth everything we have said, eaten, kissed, or vomited, in our head everything we have thought and forgotten, in our eyes all our tears and laughter, all our lights and shadows.

Think of it: every man and woman we have met, touched, or seen, sticking to us, irremovable like a little piece of adhesive tape we can't get rid of as we move it from finger to finger. Eternally aware, we would discover that we are eternally welded at every joint in our mind and body to a vast, misshapen, terrifying mass of human beings who are prisoners of one another—as in Vigeland's famous sculptured group in Oslo.

There's a real Inferno for you—wild, screaming, shrieking, streaked by lurid hatreds like lightning in the sky.

Can you offer me a hope proportionate to my Hell? I know your merchandise. In your stock you have only two articles to offer me. One is a dissolving solution that fuses all individual consciences in a kind of Nirvana. The other is an absolving solution that melts interpersonal ties and restores each one of us to our aloneness.

In effect it's the old story of a Europe of the fatherlands versus a supranational Europe. In your Christian version you favor the Europe of the fatherlands; but in your saints' communion you make a concession to supranationality.

Frankly neither formula tempts me. Perhaps you will tell me that love still remains. That's how our friend Chesterton gets out of it. Subtly contrasting cosmopolitanism and internationalism, he writes:* "International peace means a peace between nations, not a peace after the destruction of nations, like the Buddhist peace after the destruction of personality. The golden age of the good European is like the heaven of the Christian: it is a place where people will love each other; not like the heaven of the Hindu, a place where they will be each other."

Pretty good argument, don't you think? You replace the good neighbors' inevitable hatred with the good Christian's love for everyone—and that's supposed to do the trick.

I don't thing the argument is strong enough to convince me. First of all, I'd have

---

* From Chesterton's essay, "French and English" in his *All Things Considered*, Methuen, London, 1926.

to be convinced of the existence of this universal love. To love one another—precisely what does that mean? Can one love a thing or person without refusing to love another? I have no passion for the absolute or for exclusivity, but it seems to me that love is, above all, movement, direction, choice. One goes toward another person or other persons; one cannot go toward *all* other persons. There is no drawing together that doesn't assume a drawing apart. It is possible to love in many directions at the same time, but how can one love in all directions simultaneously? How can one love everything? Universal love is universal indifference. The devil understands this better than you—unless you yourself are the devil.

I realize that men's love for one another is simply the reflection of your love for them. But for goodness' sake, what meaning do you expect us to give this very love if you share it among everything in creation? You were better understood when you were the jealous God of the Old Testament. You showed preferences that justified at least your need for exclusivity. But now? One can demand a certain amount of loyalty from a customer who shops at a neighborhood store, but not from a customer who buys at chain stores.

I know, you've anticipated my objections: "Each one has his share of love and all have it entire." But then we're in the realm of miracles, with the multiplying loaves of bread. Forgive me if I can't follow you there. I'm out of my depth.

Besides, if you aren't the devil, do you love the devil? It's a basic question. I've often posed it to believers and theologians. The least one can say is that you haven't been very generous in lighting their lantern.

I would easily understand your not loving the devil. I don't love him either and I tend to prefer you. To love means to prefer. In fact, I'd almost tell you I loved you if I were sure you'd accept this kind of love— which is neither universal nor unconditional and certainly doesn't embrace all creatures. The most I'm willing to grant you is that I'm fond of all the people I don't detest, and among them are a few I love—period. If I had the same weights and measures for the rest of humanity as for those few I love, I'd feel I was betraying them.

What about you? How relieved I'd be if I

knew you had your favorites, your preferences, your prejudices! The hardest thing of
all is not to admit the harm you do to your
creatures, but to reconcile it with your
protestations of universal love.

Do you know this passage?

"A God who could make good children
as easily as bad, yet preferred to make bad
ones; who could have made every one of them
happy, yet never made a single happy one;
who made them prize their bitter life, yet
stingily cut it short; who gave his angels
eternal happiness unearned, yet required his
other children to earn it; who gave his angels
painless lives, yet cursed his other children
with biting miseries and maladies of mind
and body; who mouths justice and invented
hell—mouths mercy and invented hell—
mouths Golden Rules, and forgiveness multi-
plied by seventy times seven, and invented
hell; who mouths morals to other people and
has none himself; who frowns upon crimes,
yet commits them all; who created man without invitation, then tries to shuffle the responsibility for man's act upon man, instead of
honorably placing it where it belongs, upon
himself; and finally, with altogether divine

obtuseness, invites this poor, abused slave to worship him!..."*

It's rather harsh, I admit, and even a little unfair in spots. But you can't ignore this voice crying out in despair and rebellion. Do you know whose voice it is? Don't guess. It's a humorist named Mark Twain.

As I've told you, leftist humor doesn't always make me laugh. But—I don't know why it is—Mark Twain's terrible anger gives me truer and stronger cheer than all of Chesterton's pirouettes.

Listen to the conclusion of his statement. An angel is speaking. It's *our* revelation, and as valid as yours:

"There is no God, no universe, no human race, no earthly life, no heaven, no hell. It is all a dream—a grotesque and foolish dream. Nothing exists but you. And you are but a *thought* — a vagrant thought, a useless thought, a homeless thought, wandering forlorn among the empty eternities!"

I like that!

* From Mark Twain's *The Mysterious Stranger*.

Bordeaux, November 5-8, 1965

I hope, Sir, you're not a devotee of the magazine *Planète*. If you are, you go down in my esteem. Not that it's not an outstanding publication. In it you will find noted professors, influential political figures, famous artists, a whole array of capable, brilliant, and overworked persons—the best our technological civilization can offer.

But I'm afraid that among so many gifted minds, a simple god may seem a little dull and provincial.

Indeed, maybe you don't know *Planète*. It's less a magazine than a state of mind, just like French radical socialism,* but more cosmic. There's a *Planète* style, a *Planète* imagination, and even a *Planète* way of thinking. Depending on how you look at it, it's a theology that has gone beyond God or an atheism that has reinvented religion.

The feeling of awe which the English call "the spirit of wonder" is in men's hearts as soon as they open their eyes on life. What-

---

* Unlike its name, a moderate political movement that is barely left of center.

ever their fate, they never get fully accustomed to the extraordinary adventure of living. Even when the jail cell of organized nature, even when the cage of a police state closes in on them and keeps them imprisoned, they discover between the bars and stones clefts of time and space allowing dreams of similar universes to slip through. Naïve litany of the child chanting its nursery rhyme or science fiction of the intellectual imbued with certainties—there is always a dimension that escapes precise measurement and calculation.

For a long time you were in that zone bathed by an unreal light. Religion fed on strangeness as it provided the imagination and sensitivity with their fill of the irrational. There was even a time when the real and unreal, the natural and supernatural, the historical, epic, and legendary, the human, divine, and fantastic were all inextricably intertwined in logic-defying, indestructible monuments of architecture—as the cathedrals still bear witness. The prosaic travel diary of the Venetian Marco Polo seemed a book of miracles to his contemporaries, and the book of miracles of the mysterious Sir John Mandeville guided the first discoverers of the New World in their very real but very poetic voyages.

This was a favorable situation for you; you should have been satisfied with it. But could that be? Heads grew hard, reasons more demanding, and realities were stranger than fiction. That's when religion had to carry out its updating—only then it was called the Reformation. Nor did the Counter-Reformation lag behind. Your own servants, in their zeal, incited a clash between reason and faith that was inevitable but disastrous for your cause. If I remember correctly, the first historians to propose a critical method designed to separate legend from truth were seventeenth-century Spanish priests, Jeronimo de San José and Nicolas Antonio.

From that day on Christianity stopped consciously believing in the world of magic and buried the dream that became superstition in the deep recesses of the soul in which we hide our guilt feelings.

One last time, in the days of Charles Perrault,* the fairies donned again the

* French writer of the seventeenth century, famous for his Mother Goose tales.

hooped skirts they still wear in our imagination. Now, exiled from earth, they no longer have the leisure to keep up with the fashions of the great *couturiers*. As for witches, we retain the same images of them as when they were burned at the stake—attired in the prim, dark dresses of New England.

What a mistake you made then! If you wanted to refine faith and keep for yourself —still another sign of your jealousy—all the momentum of that impulse that thrust men toward unreal things, you should have fought your adversary in broad daylight, and not given him the advantage of an underground struggle. A fire that blazes forth is much easier to control than one that lurks underground.

Superstition, which is your tender enemy and the object of your loving disdain, has camouflaged itself with strange faces, including that of mysticism. In any outburst of passionate faith, we shall never know how much of it is rapture, divine possession, or a hysteria expressing, in half-amorous and half-theological language, the revolt of repressed dreams.

Sadist eroticism, flare-ups of Methodist

faith, cult of nature, Pamela's doubtful virginity, Manon Lescaut's charming immorality, incests hinted at and full blown, humorous eccentricities, lecheries of lascivious little priests, soothing tears of the sensitive man, diabolical games, reign of virtues, dizzy whirl of the guillotine, illuminism, esotericism, exoticism of American forests and Oriental tales, the little thrill of "black" novels, the big thrill of drugs—such were the somber and secret flowers of the century of your renunciation, the eighteenth.

The nineteenth century suffered a hangover from all that. It was called the *mal du siècle*—the sickness of the century. But a machine-based civilization brought in a new magic, the magic of Jules Verne's astronauts and Madame Blavatsky's ectoplasms, of great explorations and great Pyramids, of great scoops in journalism and the Eiffel Tower on the Champ-de-Mars— not to mention the Great War. Spiritualism and chauvinism, utopianism and humanism—there was something for every taste. Everything was included in the price of the ticket for the ideal city: free seats at every available cranny, dreams for all, the blessings of the sorcerer goddess of electricity, and the delights of a bicycle built for two. Only a few "nuts" still sought a substitute for God in adultery à la Madame Bovary, in absinthe, homosexuality, the Action Française,* or the verbal ravings of the *poètes maudits*.†

Then the joke ended. It took seventy-five years and three generations. There were three stages to the escalation: the try-out of the Paris Commune, the blow struck at Verdun, and the double blow of Auschwitz and Hiroshima. "In those machines," Camember the military engineer explains, "there are always three strokes." Three strokes, and the curtain rises on a new world, a clean, well-lit world, like Hemingway's hell.

The technocratic city has no crannies. It has substituted a crystal structure, hard and unassailable, for the human plasma of ancient societies. If someone stirs, everything trembles. The foundations are solid and the joints firmly welded, but if some-

* French royalist movement in the first decades of the twentieth century, part of the "radical Right."

† Literally, "damned poets." Originally the title of a book by Paul Verlaine (1884), this expression came to designate such poets as Rimbaud, Mallarmé, and Verlaine himself.

thing gives way the whole structure crumbles. Meanwhile after each slaughter its halls are cleansed with scouring powders, disinfectants, and deodorants; and the old scandals—poverty, oppression, and despair—are shut up in closets that have clean lines and natty colors created by the best industrial designers.

The approximate, the temporary, and the indefinite are shoved into the volcanic regions of the Third World where things are brewing with great splotches of blood. Sheltered behind his atom bombs, his washing machines, and his social security, the citizen of the technocratic city soothes his conscience by aiding underdeveloped countries and investing in humanitarian ventures; but he makes sure not to open his own doors. From time to time he extends himself and opens a gate to allow a nondescript mass of unskilled labor to enter, since machines can't do everything yet; or to take in some isolated group left high and dry by the tide of history in North Africa, Indonesia, the Congo, or elsewhere.

What does one do in such a city where even war is suicide and mutual aid a form of barter, when the spirit of wonder rebels and looks for cracks to escape through? Once again awakened to the century we live in, the Church is engaged in a self-examination comparable to that of the Reformation and Counter-Reformation. It talks of reason, common sense, the spirit of practicality; it puts on everyday clothes, strips the mass of its Latin magic and the cathedral of its sacred shadows. It is also stuffing up its cracks. It had to do so, but dreams no longer get through.

Now the horoscope makers, the faith healers, the discoverers of imaginary worlds, the observers of flying saucers have a field day. But these are rather childish games; one cannot play at them without demeaning oneself. When one is a celebrity conscious of his status or an intellectual concerned about the niceties of the mind, when one has the means to afford upper-class irrationality, when one is too old to enjoy sports cars and not old enough to be a senile voyeur, one reads *Planète* and talks himself into believing in it.

I read *Planète* and get a great deal of pleasure from it, but I don't believe in it.

Imaginative realism and science fiction seem to me excellent literary themes but not ways of confronting life. I have the greatest love and respect for literature. Only it strikes me that literature should flow from life, not the other way around. I feel some pity for those unfortunates who, in a universe in which they are bored, make frantic efforts to give a rare and strange flavor to dull everyday reality. The attempt bears a strong resemblance to the invention of Hell in the Middle Ages: Martians and astronauts are merely the modern version of horned devils. But with contemporary man it's no longer the grayness of a life that gets longer and each day starts all over again.

What a sorry way of looking at things! For the wonder of it all is that the world is a daily thing, that one day succeeds another, that the sun rises every morning and sets every evening. *My* poetry, *my* fantasy, is this day-by-dayness—freely offered and fantastic—which can have no rhyme or reason for me since I live as I do because it exists, nor can I do anything about it. I never weary of watching that ingenious machine we call your creation turn round and round. Alongside it, the perfectly useless gadgets invented by the Americans seem objects of prime necessity. Your creation is a combination of pinball machine, jukebox, and kaleidoscope. It wobbles, sputters, creaks, throws off sparks, and yet it turns. *Eppur si muove.* Dear old Galileo!

Your creation is made of solid stuff. It never misses: one and one make two, two and two make four every time—without exception. It's a true miracle, but I have faith in it. If one day it appeared to be going wrong, if suddenly I witnessed an impossible scene or an improbable happening, I would defend my right to dream by saying, like the imperturbable characters of that British caricaturist whose name escapes me, "My dear, there is certainly some very simple explanation."

In any case I wouldn't beat my brains out looking for magic in the breakdown of a motor or any other common mechanical accident. I would certainly not make any shoddy theology out of it. As Chesterton—that man again!—said, when I want a God, I know where to find him. If the day ever comes when I need magic so badly that I'm no longer content to read the daily horoscope in my hometown paper *Sud-Ouest*, I won't be satisfied with a substitute, I'll go right to your door.

Religion is like love: there are proper places for it. Religion is practiced in a church as love is made in bed. It's a question of good sense, comfort, and effectiveness.

But to a teacher of literature like myself the most flagrant nuisances are those who make love and religion in books. Love in books is not so embarrassing, but religion is a real calamity. The writer becomes a demiurge, his book a creation equal to yours, his imagination a visitation from the Holy Spirit. Reading it is like gulping down the holy wafer.

There comes a moment when the temptation to be sacrilegious becomes irresistible. I promised above to tell you what I was busy with at the end of October. I was involved in a kind of week-long seminar on art and literature organized by a few friends and myself. We were trying to revive a few intellectual corpses in Paris and Bordeaux, by confronting them with some living artists and writers on the one hand (there are still some around), and some readers, spectators and genuine lovers of culture (there are already a lot of them around), in the hope that this feeling for life would spread.

The experiment seems to have worked. The sick are stirring and, to quote our military engineer Camember once more, that's proof that the remedy works.

But what a revelation this confrontation was to me! One of the points on our agenda was relations between art and the machine. There was a kind of symbolism in it: the machine representing the technology that helps us to live, and art representing the dream that prevents us from dying.

After all I've told you, you won't be surprised to learn that the overwhelming majority of those taking part—artists, writers, critics, professors, professional authors, and well-read nonprofessionals—approached the problem with a theological mentality. But you weren't the one at issue. Some deified art, others the machine. Some confused that brilliant stroke of semantic approximation known as the artist's creation with the first chapter of Genesis and waxed indignant when anyone sought to introduce mechanical aids into the preparation and interpretation of the creative urge. The others, apparently incapable of understanding the relatively simple principle by which those highly perfected instruments, computers, function, bowed before the mighty IBM machines like primitives before fire sticks and fetishes, entreating them to turn out works of art at will.

Virtually the only ones who took the machine for what it is—a tool—and art for what it should be—a privileged language—were workers from the plant committees who had agreed to join in the experiment and for once participate in the sort of undertaking to which they are rarely invited.

Maybe it's because the machine is more useful and familiar to them than it is to intellectuals. Maybe too the thin veneer of optimism that carefully conceals the gaps and clefts in their lives in the technocratic city quickly peels and allows them a glimpse of dreams. To know the anguish of uncertainty and the bitter joys of forced leisure, they don't have to invent an unknowable or imagine the divine behind each of their gestures. All they have to do is to glance at the housewife's shopping basket or consider their employment offices.

The intellectual's problem is altogether different. Futile by vocation, sooner or later they awaken to their futility as I awakened during my lecture in Casablanca, Edinburgh, or Bilbao. Usually it happens around the age of thirty-five and is a shattering experience. Each one copes with it in his own way.

Those on whom you have shed your grace take the road of the church. Others take the same road to please their wife, thus winning a certain amount of peace and quiet in their household and gaining the respect of the local merchants. On occasion they may even nibble at a few spiritual tidbits that dulls their hunger for dreams until they die.

There are those who begin to frequent houses of ill fame, those who drift along, who drink, who gossip, who become cabinet ministers and discover the magic of power when the republic tumbles down on their head; those who aim at the Goncourt Prize, the Nobel Prize, the Legion of Honor, the French Academy, the presidency, the vice-presidency, the office of general secretary, a leading committee, a deanship, an honorary degree, a consulship, a proconsulship, or what have you. They peer intently when they see themselves in a mirror and then avert their faces from the reproach in their deadened eyes.

There are those who become Freemasons, join the Soka Gakkai,* Moral Rearmament, or Opus Dei movement, and seem to get along nicely.

There are the sports lovers—but that passion only lasts until the middle-age spread.

There are the political activists. I admire them. From a distance and without being able to imitate them. The world of committees and slogans is even more hermetic than that of technocracy. One needs extraordinary agility to slip into their clefts and an iron will to drill holes in them. The only exits open to all are treason or death. I happen to like neither the one nor the other.

There are those who commit suicide. They are rare. One usually does that at an earlier age, when a thirst for the absolute

---

* Contemporary Japanese religious-political movement, offshoot of a Buddhist sect, and strongly nationalist in tone.

still prevails.

There are those who read *Planète*.

And then there are all the others who muddle through. They remind me of a story Roger Caillois* told me in Vera Cruz one day when he had put more rum than sherry in his drink.

In Japan, he said, there is a temple whose priests have but one function. They walk around the building chanting: "What we are engaged in doing is good for something!"

---

* Contemporary French writer, author of many literary and philosophical studies.

I'm furious, sir, about this holiday. Being a Thursday, it deprives my students of their scheduled class on Hell in literature. I hope you'll bear that in mind during their final exams.

It's your fault too. Didn't you plainly state that we should let the dead bury the dead? Well, can't you get people to obey you?

Here too you might usefully have demonstrated your divine jealousy. How is it you've never been able to do away with this cult of the dead, which in reality is nothing but a cult of self? Giraudoux said it before me, and much better than I can express it: there's a kind of indecency about paying tributes to the dead, which they can easily get along without, and asking them to consecrate the petty vanity of the living. Veterans gather at war memorials on the pretext of commemorating the dead; what they are really there for is to find reasons for believing they haven't suffered in vain.

I know, the butchery in World War I, the first in modern times—at least the first that couldn't be ignored—was such a traumatic event to the generation it struck that the survivors have a right to every excuse. But to us, men of the following generation, slaughter became a familiar thing. We know now that the beast in us has not been slain by civilization, reason, and science—as for a time we had hoped. Quite the contrary, we know that it has found weapons hitherto beyond its reach. We know that the reawakenings of the beast have been more and more horrible.

All of World War I caused fewer deaths than the German concentration camps of World War II alone. In a few minutes at Hiroshima and Nagasaki, in a few hours at Dresden and Hamburg, the Allies destroyed more human lives than the American armies lost in the course of two world wars. World War I killed one Frenchman and one German out of thirty. World War II killed one German in fourteen and one Soviet citizen in ten.

I'm not quoting all these figures to overwhelm you. You're not responsible; in fact, I know you yourself would prefer to kill us by natural causes. But I'm trying to show you why Veterans Day—November 11—no longer has much meaning for a man of my age and experiences.

You may tell me that one can think of the war dead without making a cult of it, and that day is just as good as any other. Meteorologically, November 11 is a better date than, say, June 8. Autumn is a fitter season for mourning.

Sir, you are very kind—but why only that day and that season? Do you think my mind has ever forgotten what my eyes have seen? Not that I have seen so much ... but the look of a friend disappearing in the night and fog; a familiar face transformed into a mask of horror; my father slowly dying for forty years from the effects of poison gas, and dying as he lived, a smile and a cigarette on his lips.

Do you think I need monuments to think about them, to be with them at every moment of my life and forever? Flags, bugles, speeches, all the hubbub surrounding the cult of the dead embarrasses me more than they help me. As for the minute of silence, all I ever could think about during those interminable seconds was the big toe on my left foot that was cold and the ant crawling over my neck.

Yet I dutifully attend the Veterans Day ceremony at my university because there are still many World War I veterans left; and, out of love for them, I want to make the only gesture that can convey my solidarity with them. I go there for the living, not the dead.

So here I am again beneath the Bordeaux sky, a low gray sky like one of Mauriac's consciences. I'm not sorry I went to the ceremony. It took place, as it does every year, in front of Montaigne's grave. The tomb contains a few bones that are said to be a woman's. It seems that someone made a mistake when the remains were transferred. Below ground level lies the stone coffin embedded in the concrete of an old German shelter, and a laboratory bench has been sealed up in the wall.

Tell that to Montaigne if he's with you (which is doubtful). I think it will give him pleasure. He was so worried about dying well and, all in all, managed to live not too badly. He'll like the idea of still being involved with human life.

But I didn't see you this morning. Do you sometimes appear in front of war memorials in cemeteries? Do you measure in human terms what, in your eyes, is simply the passage from one state to another?

I doubt it; and maybe it's better so. You call yourself the living God and that's a good thing. If you want to honor that sublime title, no one will complain. Busy yourself with life, but do a good job. Don't make it a trap, a temptation, or a bargain basement. Give it its chance. That's all I ask of you.

As for us, we do after all have to look after our dead. Not because of their death but because of the life they possessed and then lost, but also handed down, safeguarded, affirmed, and sometimes improved. This short-lived fate, this ability to reach out from wave to wave for the inaccessible, in a tide that dies with each breaker but rises again with each new wave—these are the only things we possess and which you will never possess.

You will never possess them because you are alone and unique in your three persons; because, despite all myths and symbols, you are not married. I realize that I have written you a man-to-man letter, no doubt because I'm of the male sex and you are a virile God.

I ought to have talked more about women with you. In them is embodied that *élan vital*, that driving force of the species so dear to German philosophers, which transcends the individual and his brief ambitions. Men are dead limbs, blind alleys, stagnant pools. Women are living waters. Goethe's Faust is wrong when he says the Eternal Feminine draws us on high; in reality, it carries us along and hurls us at the horizon like a flood tide.

In his play *Man and Superman*, Shaw shows us a Don Juan who wants to be a superman, but Doña Ana replies to him that she is looking for a father for the superman. It ends badly, of course, since ultimately both of them come together again in Heaven. In my view Shaw was wrong. Don Juan's place is really in Heaven where he will find all the superhuman qualities men are so fond of. But Doña Ana's place is on earth where, from cradle to cradle, from coffin to coffin, women drive us, like a reluctant but acquiescent flock, toward the man of tomorrow which we shall never be. For so long as time remains and you have the good sense not to stop the clock, today will never be tomorrow.

Let's talk seriously. The situation is beginning to be serious. The more I go along, the less I can imagine you engaged in reading my letter. True, if we can believe what they say, maybe you're reading it right now, not only over my shoulder but even inside my head. And in my head you're reading it twice: once at the moment in which my mind directs my hand and once when my eye, following my hand, indicates to my mind that its orders have been carried out. Between the two there is a lag of a few hundredths of a second and, what is more annoying, a certain number of differences caused by the imperfections in the tools I use—pen, language, hand, brain, paper. There must be some frightful discordances betwen them, like two guitar strings out of tune.

At the same time I imagine you must look upon everything I've wanted to write, tried to write, refused to write, renounced writing, everything I could have, should have, and haven't written, as more or less remote harmonies. To you the tenuous thread of my expressed thoughts is but a mite lost in the vast skein of possibilities.

Indeed, I get lost in it myself because in that realm no one can unwind the Ariadne thread all alone. One needs an accomplice, a silent but present listener. A reader is a little like a writer's psychoanalyst.

One may explore by himself the moving labyrinth of the conscience, but as soon as he wishes to penetrate its murky corners, light up its darkest recesses, and look for underground escape routes, he needs someone who listens to him, reads him, and accompanies him on the dangerous journey as Virgil accompanied Dante.

Then the golden thread of speech unwinds. Usually, I admit, it turns out to be an ordinary piece of string. But at least one can grab hold of it, though not without danger. Sometimes it slackens and the explorer, cut off from his companion, gets lost. Sometimes it grows too taut and the explorer remains in one spot, prisoner of his cord.

With you I have too many threads to follow, some too taut, some too slack. So I grope like a blind man, constantly retracing my steps, finding at every turning the wall I had stumbled against the moment before. I contradict myself, disavow myself, perjure myself from line to line, fearing lest suddenly I should see the formidable Minotaur loom up at the end of the corridor.

In this instance the Minotaur is the philosopher or theologian whose territory I have recklessly invaded; who, having grown up in the labyrinth, knows all its ins and outs and has a good time watching me go around and around. The horned beast is well armed, and my only weapon of defense is my passionate zeal. At the first clash I shall bite the dust.

Yet it's not the Minotaur that worries me most. It's you, your absence. This is the first time I have ever talked this way to an intangible, perhaps nonexistent, reader, whose reality dissolves as I launch my fitful verbal assaults at him. Usually I feel my readers around me and am borne along by the outbursts of rage or laughter caused by my words. I don't feel you, I'm not borne along by you. Really, I think you're the worst audience I've ever had.

The other readers—those for whom this book is being published—can't help me out at all. They will be the indifferent, amused, sarcastic, or infuriated witnesses of my pir-

ouettes and turnabouts; but they will not
take part in the cruel game going on between
me alone and absent you.

This is my twenty-fifth book. To cele-
brate the occasion, I've indulged in the expensive luxury of a duet with emptiness. I've
done it for myself, fully aware of all the
risks. If I emerge victorious from the labyrinth, I won't even be aware of it. I only know
I've done what I wanted to do for a long time.
For the first time in my life, it matters little
to me whether I receive cheers or boos.

Some assignment!

"A little letter to God," Robert Sabatier
said coaxingly to me, "why, you can dash it
off during your vacation."

My vacation is long since over, yet I
haven't finished with you. I won't be finished
with you when I've completed this book.
After the manuscript is sent to the publisher
and my papers put in order, you'll still be
there, before me, on my table, on my fountain
pen, on my typewriter keys, in my hand, absent yet haunting me. No one is more present
in absence than you.

You see where my boldness has led me.
I'm no more interested now than I was before

in the question of your existence, but I can no longer ignore the little game of hide and seek we're playing—you and I. It's always dangerous to evoke ghosts. One never knows how to make them disappear again. It matters little whether you are the more or less morbid figment of my anxiety or a real entity making fun of my imaginings.

The fact is the dialogue I have begun with you will only end with my death.

Perhaps too only with my death will it really begin, if perchance you are wily enough to exist. Then I'll know if the mailman delivered my letter to you and whether there's any reply. For the moment you are silent. Nor would I be surprised to get my letter back with a notice stamped on it: "ADDRESS UNKNOWN." That's a shame. Should the day ever come when we meet face to face, promise me that you in turn will tell me what you have to say.

But, for pity's sake, take all the time you want. I'm in no hurry.